MW00564767

matcha
meets
macaron

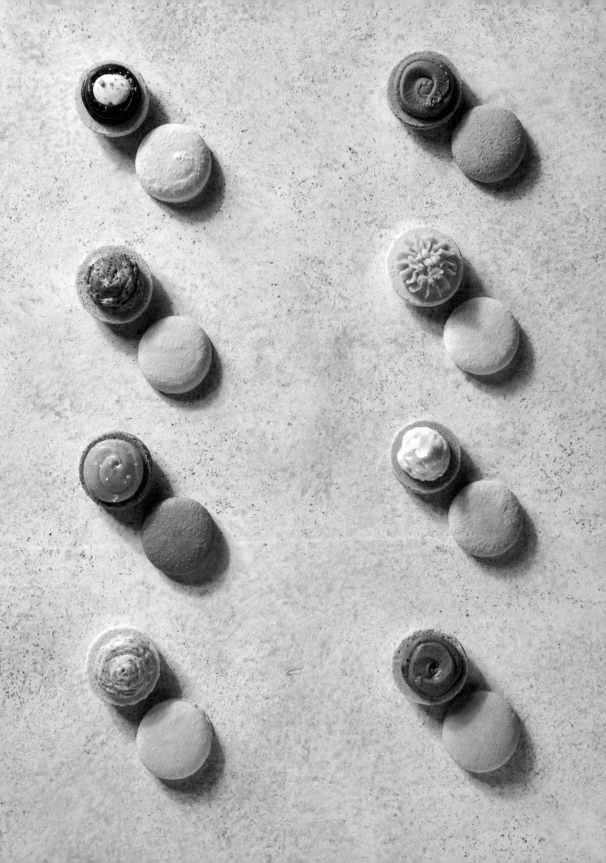

matcha meets macaron

SWEET TREATS WITH AN ASIAN FLAIR

Lisa He

Photography by **KARA CHIN**

Countryman Press

An Imprint of W. W. Norton & Company
Independent Publishers Since 1923

Copyright © 2024 by Borderlands Bakery, LLC
Photography copyright © 2024 by Kara Chin
Photography on pages xii, xiii, 27, 28, and 31 © 2024 by James d'Shone

All rights reserved
Printed in China

For information about permission to reproduce selections from this book, write to
Permissions, Countryman Press, 500 Fifth Avenue, New York, NY 10110

For information about special discounts for bulk purchases, please contact
W. W. Norton Special Sales at specialsales@wwnorton.com or 800-233-4830

Manufacturing by Toppan Leefung Pte. Ltd.
Book design by Suze Myers
Art director: Allison Chi
Production manager: Devon Zahn

Countryman Press
www.countrymanpress.com

An imprint of W. W. Norton & Company, Inc.
500 Fifth Avenue, New York, NY 10110
www.wwnorton.com

978-1-68268-828-1

10 9 8 7 6 5 4 3 2 1

For my parents and grandma,

**WHO SACRIFICED SO MUCH
SO I GET TO BE ME**

Contents

Introduction

My family didn't decorate Christmas cookies or make brownies for school bake sales. I didn't grow up baking, and my special childhood memories don't involve cooking with a grandmother, either. Baking didn't become part of my life until college.

I was born in Shanghai in 1988, and when I was 10 months old, my dad went to America. A few years later, my mom joined him. I stayed behind, and my extended family did an incredible job of taking care of me. My dad called every month and sent Snickers bars and other chocolates from Costco, which hadn't opened in China yet. As my extended family and I savored the sweets, they told me that I would have unlimited access to Snickers after I joined my parents in the States. In the meantime, endless construction and the tantalizing aromas of food surrounded me everywhere in Shanghai, in the streets and at home. Every family gathering, big or small, celebrated eating. We all contributed and enjoyed the fruits of our labor. Every meal gave us the opportunity to spend time together and share a common love for food.

Just as my aunts had promised me, I reunited with my parents at age six. My mom collected me from China, and we flew on a double-decker airplane to San Francisco. Seeing my dad for practically the first time felt strange. We had talked on the phone every month, but interacting with him in person came as a whole new experience. It scared us both a little. So did acclimating to America, which, for me, required long, confusing days of trying to fit in, awkwardly making friends, enduring Hooked on Phonics sessions with my dad after school,

struggling with math homework designed for kids older than me, and reciting short stories to my parents in English to earn stickers. We rarely dined out, eating almost every meal in the makeshift kitchen: a laundry room outfitted with a burner and sink. We sat around a table bought from a garage sale, on which my mom served mostly Chinese dishes, such as sautéed vegetables and steamed fish, pork, or tofu. Attending the family dinner was mandatory, and I loved it. As a special treat, my dad occasionally took me to McDonald's for McChicken sandwiches and fries, a huge splurge at the time. Those positive core memories formed my love for fast food, which, for better or worse, still exists today.

When I turned seven, Grandma, dad's mom, joined us to take care of cooking, cleaning, and chaperoning me to and from school so my parents could concentrate on building a better life for us. Grandma made delicious meals, but she never involved me

in the process. The adults worked together so I could focus on school and my new life in a new country.

At age 12, I noticed some AOL CDs in a pile of junk mail, and they connected me to the Internet, where I discovered K-pop chat forums. My parents knew nothing about the genre, but thankfully they let me pursue the interest. Americans wanted K-pop merch and lots of it, which inspired me to create custom bookmarks. I asked my dad for a printer and laminator so that I could make them to sell online, which gave me money to buy posters, CDs, Sanrio grab bags, and of course fast food. That experience gave me my first taste of entrepreneurship.

My parents bought their first home in the East Bay as I was entering high school. The kitchen had a dishwasher and oven, but we didn't know what to do with those

appliances, so they served as storage. In college, I studied biomedical engineering while running a handmade jewelry business, which made me desperately crave an outlet to relieve stress. As a sophomore, I moved into an apartment, which, for the first time, gave me access to an empty, functioning oven. My roommates and I roasted chicken and baked pasta in it, but it still hadn't dawned on me that it could make desserts.

On a whim, I decided to try my hand at blueberry muffins, sourcing the recipe from a blog. It worked, and that success led me to cookies, cheesecakes, and more. I brought extra baked goods with me to class, leaving them outside lecture halls with no note, no explanation. They disappeared quickly. The next year, an ad for macarons popped onto my computer screen. They captured my imagination. But my new obsession unwittingly landed on one of the hardest desserts

to make. At the time, I hadn't yet discovered baking by weight, gauging oven temperature, or understanding the importance of environment or technique. Almond flour isn't cheap, either, especially for college students, so I had to ration it and other expensive ingredients. Batches of macaron batter failed, but the pain of the chase became part of the thrill. Baking to relieve stress, it turned out, gave me a lot of kitchen know-how and confidence.

A biotech gig in 2011 challenged me and played perfectly into the trope of model minority. It didn't pay much, but a stable job in a bad economy felt like a blessing. In October of that year, the company hosted a bake sale for National Breast Cancer Awareness Month. A coworker asked me to make a sugar-free cookie. Without hesitating, I agreed, but I had *no* idea what I'd committed to doing.

Sugar substitutes and baking with them have come a long way since 2011. Instead of a guided rolling pin, which I didn't have yet, I used a wine bottle. That bake sale request led me to sugar cookies . . . and the embarrassment of assuming that people decorated them with colored egg wash! But without that request, I ultimately wouldn't have written this book, so there's something to be said for feeling uncomfortable and being bad at something but trying anyway. "Try again. Fail again. Fail better," as playwright Samuel Beckett put it. My colleagues paid $3 each for sugar-free "sugar" cookies made with saccharine and slathered with pink egg wash. The cookies raised money for a good cause, and they encourage me to encourage you. They also brought me to Amber Spiegel of SweetAmbs, who introduced me to the world of cookie decorating.

Baking helped calm me while navigating corporate life. My dessert experiments and extras started conversations and helped build relationships. At first, my shyness convinced me just to leave the cookies in common areas, but people asked who made them. Word got around that they came from the kid outside the VP's office. Coworkers and their friends asked me to make more for birthdays and baby showers. Colleagues eagerly anticipated them in meetings. Almost everyone who visited my cubicle knew that I was moonlighting as a baker. I was smart, good at my job, and nice, but cookies always sweetened the deal. In many ways, they helped advance my career.

But by 2013, the hobby was costing a lot of money. To cover ingredient costs, I started selling on Etsy and Facebook. Selling to strangers, a trial by fire, taught me a lot: volume at scale, schedules and workflows, packaging and shipping. My learning-curve failures—preventing butter bleed, shipping sugar cookies safely, managing a cottage bakery—disappointed some people. But inside each experience lay a valuable lesson. Luckily, lots of understanding customers gave me the opportunity to get it right.

No two people have the same experience, equipment, environment, or techniques. We all start from distinct baselines and troubleshoot problems differently. To share my journey and findings with others, I posted my bakes and thoughts on Instagram. People slowly but steadily gravitated toward my content, starting another kind of cookie relationship in my life. The more I posted, the more people expressed their curiosity about how I did what I did. They unexpectedly loved the behind-the-scenes, often mundane aspects of running a little cookie business.

For years, climbing the corporate ladder occupied my days, and baking, maybe working out, and spending quality time with my dogs and ex-husband filled the evenings. The natural high of producing little edible works of art helped me survive a not-great average of four or five hours of sleep each night. But all that time and effort paid off with the incredible experiences of appearing on Food Network and Netflix. My baking business was growing, as was my tech career, which left little time for anything else, including family and friends. As a result of this demanding schedule, my personal life took a hit, and I had to take a step back to revisit my priorities. We all navigate difficult seasons of life, and I am grateful for challenging experiences because each built who I am today. If you're open to a bit of advice, take the time to determine what

matters most to your authentic self *and* what balance means to you. The community that has formed around Borderlands Bakery finds inspiration in my bakes and looks to me for insights, and not just related to baking! This is a huge honor that I never expected and that I take very seriously. That trust matters to me, so I treat it with loving care.

This book represents the culmination of my cultures, baking experiences, and personal/professional growth. Through my recipes, I pay tribute to the people who have impacted my life—colleagues at my first biotech company, people who supported me through the late nights, and those whom I've inspired to get into baking so they can continue spreading the joy that

baked goods bring. The nontraditional path of baking as a full-time career allowed me to found and run two companies: Borderlands Bakery, which offers cookies, classes, and supplies, and My Custom Bakes, which provides order-management software for cottage bakeries.

Matcha Meets Macaron follows my baking journey, from beginner-friendly bakes, through the macarons and other cookies that I made and that made me, to the new confections that celebrate my heritage and upbringing. If you enjoy the recipes in this book or want to share the challenges and triumphs of your own baking adventures, please connect with me on social media or at BorderlandsBakery.com.

Life is short, so bake it sweet!

Kitchen Staples

Keep the following ingredients in your refrigerator or pantry so you can whip something up if someone comes over or you want to bake for a last-minute event or occasion.

- **Baking powder and baking soda** work as leavening agents, but each behaves slightly differently. Baking soda contains pure sodium bicarbonate, which affects rise and spread. Baking powder also contains acid and cornstarch, making it less potent than baking soda. Baking powder usually provides more rise than spread, which matters for cake-like consistency and texture. Some recipes call for both because of how the molecules behave together, how long they remain active, and their interactions with other ingredients. When purchasing baking powder, look for aluminum-free formulations, which the package will indicate. Some people can taste aluminum easily and will experience an off-putting metallic flavor.

- **Butter,** whether salted or unsalted, can cause heated arguments among bakers. Using unsalted butter allows you to control the total amount of salt in a recipe more easily because different brands of salted butter contain different amounts of sodium. I started with Kirkland salted butter, a Costco brand. This butter has served me well, apart from shortbread and other butter-forward treats that require higher-quality butter, specialty butter, or less salt. Use whichever style you prefer, and if you don't like the result, try the other style. In addition to differ-

ent levels of sodium, different brands also contain different percentages of fat and moisture, which will affect your bakes. To convert unsalted butter to salted, add ¼ teaspoon kosher salt to every 4 ounces butter (1 stick).

- **Cooking spray** will make your life easier, I promise. If you're baking in pans without liners, you absolutely need it. Use any vegetable oil with a high flash point and neutral flavor, such as avocado, canola, or vegetable, or a baking spray, such as Baker's Joy or Pam. If you want to make your own, combine 1 tablespoon melted unsalted butter with 1½ teaspoons all-purpose flour. Scale as needed.

- **Cream of tartar,** also called potassium bitartrate, occurs naturally in grapes, comes from making wine, and does a *lot* in the kitchen. It stabilizes egg whites, adds tang, supports chewiness, and discourages sugar from crystallizing.

- **Eggs,** unless you have a different preference, mean regular large eggs. They get the job done.

- **Flours** come in lots of varieties, but all-purpose plays such a central role in baking that no perfect 1:1 substitute exists. Bakers can get super nerdy about the gluten and other constituents of various brands, but, if you're a beginner baker, whatever all-purpose variety that you can find most easily will work just fine. I've used the Kirkland brand forever with no issues. Cake flour has less gluten (wheat protein) than all-purpose, which usually results in a softer bake with a finer crumb structure. Cake flour also contains cornstarch.

- **Fruit,** such as dried apricots, mangoes, cranberries, and raisins, often comes in handy, so keep a selection on hand.

- **Milk** means whole cow milk, which adds moisture and richness and affects texture. You can sub your milk of choice, but this isn't an allergen-focused cookbook. Baseline the recipe with full-fat dairy the first time, then experiment to suit your taste preferences or dietary needs.

- **Nuts** for baking—almonds, macadamias, pecans, pistachios, walnuts—should be roasted and unsalted unless you have a strong preference for a different permutation.

- **Salt** for baking falls into two types: kosher, which works for most needs, and a coarse flaky salt, such as Maldon, for finishing.

- **Sugar** comes in lots of varieties—granulated white, brown, and confectioners' or powdered—and it never hurts to keep all three on hand. Granulated white is most common. Dark brown has a higher molasses content than light brown, which affects taste and texture, making it my preference for baking. Frosting, macarons, and some other cookies call specifically for confectioners' sugar.

- **Vanilla bean paste** suspends the teeny, speckly beans from a vanilla pod in a viscous syrup. It has a deeper flavor than extract and costs significantly more. For vanilla bean paste, the brand matters because lower-quality products cut the paste by grinding the whole pod. Look for Nielsen-Massey, my preferred brand.

- **Vanilla extract** soaks the beans in alcohol, which gives baked goods a sweet aroma and can enhance flavor. There's not much difference among brands, so use whatever you find most accessible, but look for pure extract and avoid anything with vanillin or other artificial flavors, which some people may find off-putting.

Specialty Ingredients

You might not be able to find all these items at your local grocery story, but many Asian grocery stores carry them, as does Amazon. Check out my Borderlands Bakery store-front at Amazon.com/shop/Borderlands Bakery and click the Matcha Meets Macaron list for links to these ingredients.

- **Chili crisp oil,** if you like some heat, adds a great element of surprise to desserts. Top vanilla ice cream with it or let it work wonders in savory macarons (page 45). If you don't like spicy, skip it.

- **Coconut milk,** especially the full-fat variety, has beautiful flavor and makes a great dairy substitute. If you don't like the flavor of coconut, use unsweetened cashew or soy milk, both of which taste creamy. Don't bother with almond milk, though, which doesn't have enough body or texture for baked goods.

- **Glutinous rice flour,** made from short-grain rice, appears widely in Asian baking. It looks indistinguishable from regular rice flour, but it has a different texture and behaves differently. Used as the base for mochi foods, it tastes a little sweeter and can feel very sticky. Despite the confusing name, it doesn't contain gluten because "gluten" specifically means wheat protein. Look for the Mochiko brand.

- **Matcha** *without* added sugars or fillers can prove hard to find, but it's worth the effort. Look for culinary-grade matcha, designed for use in cooking rather than drinking.

- **Red bean paste, or adzuki paste,** should be easy to find in cans or pouches in an Asian grocery store, and buying it beats cooking and mashing the beans yourself. Most store-bought adzuki paste already contains sugar, so taste before making modifications.

- **Salted egg yolks** have become popular in Western cuisine recently. They taste super savory, which nicely balances sweets. You can buy them in powder form, but Salted Egg Yolks are easy to make (page 53) with leftover yolks from macarons and meringues.

- **Sesame seeds,** when toasted, have a stronger fragrance and flavor than if untoasted. I keep both black and white toasted seeds on hand. Each has a slightly different taste, and they complement each other so well.

- **Ube extract** has become such a popular flavor in recent years. Keep a bottle or two in your pantry to flavor macarons, cookies, cakes, and more.

Environment, Equipment, and Definitions

Every household has a different environment, meaning a different elevation, temperature, humidity, and so forth. The use of air-conditioning or heating can affect your bakes, too. For me, "room temperature" means 68°F in winter but 78°F in summer. My college bestie keeps her home at 65°F almost year-round. Knowing your environmental parameters will save you a lot of frustration when you troubleshoot.

If you have good technique and follow a recipe to the letter but aren't achieving the desired results, assess all possibilities, including elements of your environment. Perhaps the problem lies with your equipment. Different bakeware—ceramic, glass, silicone—behaves differently. Maybe your hand mixer is breaking your meringue rather than making it.

Some people at the gym record themselves to review their form. You can't know how fast you're running unless you track it, and the same principle applies to baking—and lots of other areas of life. When I was riding the macaron struggle bus, I did exactly that, recording myself on video. Those recordings revealed a laundry list of baking sins. For batter consistency, I didn't stop at "lava flow." For the cookie base, I wasn't knocking enough air from the meringue. Piping at an angle caused lopsided results. My techniques lacked consistency. The recordings enabled me to correct these errors.

Building self-awareness matters because it will help you troubleshoot. If something isn't working, strategically evaluate your environment, equipment, and techniques.

On the positive side of the equation, if an idea strikes but you don't know whether it'll work, test it. Don't fear experimentation. But make sure to write down exactly what you do or what you change. This method will allow you to replicate the experiment or learn from it!

Equipment

You can make pretty much anything with these basic tools.

- **Baking liners or mats** prevent your bakes from sticking to pans and sheets. They come in a variety of materials, including parchment, silicone, and Teflon. Whichever you use, you should understand how each affects temperature, time, and texture. Silicone, usually the thickest of them, conducts heat the slowest, but it varies from brand to brand. In the middle comes Teflon and then parchment. Experiment and see which material you prefer for which recipe.

- **Baking or cookie sheets** provide a stable surface for your bakes. Baking sheets are rectangular with a lip around the entire pan, and cookie sheets are flat with no lip. We use baking sheets for our cookies and prefer aluminum ones such as Nordic Ware, which weigh very little and conduct heat quite evenly.

- **Cooling racks** sound like a good idea, but they can change the texture of baked goods, such as making chocolate chip cookies and bread drier or crispier. Unless you prefer a more crisp or dry texture, it's usually easier and better to cool your bakes in the baking vessel—unless a recipe specifically calls for a cooling rack.

- **Food scales,** an absolute must for consistent bakes, will change your life. Old-fashioned American baking uses volumetric measurements—teaspoons, tablespoons, cups. But dry ingredients settle differently, which can create a 20 percent margin of error! Measurement by weight is much more accurate and allows for better consistency when scaling. You usually don't need to weigh baking powder, baking soda, granulated sugar, or salt, though, because they tend to settle consistently. If you use an electronic food scale, always keep a backup battery on hand in case you suddenly need to replace a dying or dead one in the middle of a recipe.

- **Hand mixers** work well for smaller batches of thinner batters, but they're not as great for roll-out cookie dough. They can cause unintended problems with meringues in particular. Recipe instructions will indicate when you can or should use one.

- **Measuring cups and spoons** also come in lots of styles and materials, but pretty much anything will work just fine. I use stainless steel because it looks good and cleans easily.

- **Muffin and/or cupcake tins** distribute heat differently, depending on their color. Darker tins result in browner bottoms, lighter tins in lighter bottoms.

- **Oven thermometers** will tell you whether your oven runs hot, to scale, or cold. Some ovens miss by as much as 50 degrees—a total game changer! For instance, if you're baking cutout cookies but they spread too much, use an oven thermometer to check the temperature. If it's running cold, your cookies won't set as fast as they should.

- **Rolling pins** have evolved. If you need to maintain strictly consistent thicknesses, use a guided rolling pin, which features handy, adjustable thickness discs.

- **Silicone spatulas,** when made in one continuous piece without grooves, make for easy cleanup. They're also a lot easier on your hands and don't cause splinters.

- **Stand mixers** are a must-have. Look for Breville (pricier), Cuisinart (some budget-friendly models), or KitchenAid brands.

- **Storage containers** should be airtight for keeping extras and leftovers fresh. The brand doesn't matter much, but the Rubbermaid Brilliance line is my favorite.

- **Whisks** are essential. Find a couple in different sizes, simple and basic.

You'll see that I don't list a food processor (because I don't own one). It can come in handy, sure, but you won't need one for what we're doing.

Definitions

For consistency, all recipes in this book give **measurements by weight** first and then, for anyone preferring the old-fashioned style, by volume.

   Room temperature differs in every home. So what does it mean? *The American Heritage Dictionary of the English Language* gives a range: "around 20 to 22°C (68 to 72°F)." For baking, your home's ambient temperature should result in butter soft enough to leave a slight indentation when touched but not melty or oily. If you keep your home on the cooler side, lots of microwaves now feature butter-warming shortcuts. If your appliance doesn't have that feature, the easiest way to soften butter is to microwave it in 5-second increments, flipping it 90 degrees each time, for a total of 25 or 30 seconds, depending on your microwave's wattage. You also can cut the butter into chunks to increase the surface area exposed to air, which will bring it to room temperature faster, around 10 to 15 minutes. For room temperature eggs, remove them from the fridge about 1 hour before using.

   Most ovens have hot spots, meaning that ovens don't conduct heat evenly. For more consistent bakes, a lot of my recipes instruct you to **rotate your sheet** halfway through baking, which means turning your baking vessel 180 degrees so the back of the vessel moves to the front of the oven and vice versa.

1

Beginner-Friendly Bakes

When I was learning to bake, I preferred recipes that used accessible ingredients, required minimal equipment, utilized low-risk techniques, and came together relatively quickly. Let's start with some of those!

Madeleines with Matcha White Chocolate

My dad loves madeleines, which I learned to make to reconnect with him when I was in my early 20s. The perfect treat, they have reasonable portions and great texture but don't taste too sweet—more cake than cookie. This recipe isn't perfectly traditional, but it comes together quickly, produces a beautiful result with the iconic hump, and tastes delicious. Pair the cookies with or dip them in white chocolate flavored with matcha or ube extract for a new twist on a timeless classic.

PREP TIME: 10 minutes

COOK TIME: 9 minutes, plus cooling time

TOTAL TIME: 25 minutes

MAKES: 12 madeleines

OCCASIONS: potlucks, bake sales, high tea, Christmas

FOR THE MADELEINES

85 grams (6 tablespoons) salted butter

Neutral nonstick cooking spray

1 large egg, room temperature

65 grams (⅓ cup) granulated white sugar

1 teaspoon vanilla bean paste

100 grams (⅔ cup) all-purpose flour, sifted

½ teaspoon baking powder

1 teaspoon lemon or orange zest (optional)

FOR THE MATCHA WHITE CHOCOLATE

100 grams (1 cup) white chocolate chips

1 teaspoon matcha, sifted

1 For the madeleines: Microwave the butter on high for 30 seconds to melt. Let it cool to room temperature.

2 While the butter is cooling, preheat the oven to 350°F (177°C) and spray a madeleine pan with cooking spray.

3 In the bowl of a stand mixer fitted with the whisk attachment or using a hand mixer in a medium mixing bowl, beat the egg and sugar on medium speed until the mixture lightens in texture and color, 2 to 3 minutes.

4 Add the vanilla bean paste and whisk to incorporate.

5 Sift the flour and baking powder into the mixture and, with a spatula, mix until just combined.

6 Drizzle in the melted butter and citrus zest if using. Stir until just incorporated.

7 In heaping tablespoons, spoon the batter into the center of the madeleine molds.

8 Bake until the sides of the madeleines turn slightly golden and the centers have risen and spring back when gently pressed, 8 to 9 minutes.

9 While the madeleines are baking, make the matcha white chocolate. In a microwave-safe bowl, microwave the white chocolate chips on medium-high (level 7 of 10) for 1 minute.

10 Let the chips stand for 2 minutes, stir, and repeat for 30-second intervals until the chocolate fully melts.

11 Stir the matcha into the melted white chocolate.

(recipe continues)

NOTE

Madeleines taste best fresh from the oven, but, in an airtight container, they stay fresh in the fridge for 1 week and will keep in the freezer for 2 months.

12   When the madeleines finish baking, remove them from the oven and let them cool for 5 minutes.

13   Serve warm after drizzling with or dipping in matcha white chocolate, or transfer to a cooling rack to cool to room temperature to serve plain.

14   To create the molded chocolate shells design on the madeleine, into a silicone madeleine mold, pour 2 teaspoons of the hot matcha white chocolate and press the front of the madeleine into it. Chill in the fridge for 10 minutes before carefully removing.

VARIATIONS

Try adding ¼ cup of crushed chocolate sandwich cookies to switch up the flavor and texture. For Ube White Chocolate, omit the vanilla bean paste from the cookies and substitute the matcha in the coating with 1 teaspoon of ube extract. After baking, drizzle with white chocolate for a boost of sweetness that complements the ube nicely.

Red Bean Puff Pastry Cookies

I get it. Beans don't mean "dessert" for many non-Asian Americans. But in China and many parts of East Asia, red bean—known as adzuki in Japanese—reigns as one of the most versatile, beloved dessert ingredients. When I was growing up, my mom always tried to sneak red beans into my food, insisting that "it's good for women," which, as an ungrateful teenager, I dismissed as superstitious nonsense. Years later, some research revealed that, according to traditional Chinese medicine, red beans reduce fluid retention and promote clear skin. These cookies honor my mom and thank her for never giving up on me, even when I had the worst attitude. Store-bought puff pastry gives a crisp bite and fluffy texture to these easy-to-make pastries that remind me of the much more complicated versions that we used to eat at the local Chinese bakery.

PREP TIME: 15 minutes
COOK TIME: 20 minutes, plus cooling time
TOTAL TIME: 45 minutes
MAKES: 12 cookies
OCCASIONS: Chinese New Year, Mid-Autumn Festival

One 9¾-by-10½-inch sheet puff pastry, thawed in the refrigerator

125 grams (½ cup) sweetened red bean paste

1 egg

Toasted sesame seeds of choice

> **NOTE**
> You can use black or white sesame seeds, or both, for this recipe.

1 Preheat the oven to 375°F (190°C).

2 Remove the puff pastry from the fridge and let it come to room temperature for 10 minutes to make it easier to handle.

3 On a lightly floured surface, unfold the puff pastry.

4 Spread the red bean paste evenly over the puff pastry, leaving a ½-inch border around the edges.

5 Starting at one of the shorter ends, roll the puff pastry up tightly, like a jelly roll.

6 Slice the puff pastry log into 12 equal pieces.

7 Onto two baking sheets lined with parchment paper, place six rolls each, leaving plenty of room for them to puff and spread.

8 In a small bowl, beat the egg and use a pastry brush to brush it over the raw cookies.

9 Onto the cookies, sprinkle sesame seeds to taste.

10 Bake until the cookies puff and turn golden brown, 15 to 20 minutes.

11 Remove the cookies from the oven, let them cool on the baking sheet for 5 minutes, then transfer to a wire rack to cool completely.

(recipe continues)

TIPS: In step 6, to create clean, even slices, use a knife to score guidelines into the top of the log. Carefully place a piece of unflavored dental floss underneath the roll and wrap it around to the top, aligning it with the first guideline. Bring the ends of the floss together, cross them, and pull so the floss cuts through the dough.

These cookies lose their crunchy texture after about 24 hours, so enjoy them right away. You can freeze the unbaked cookies for 2 months in an airtight container.

VARIATIONS

This recipe calls for rolling the cookies up like a jelly roll, but you can shape them however you like for a different look. You also can swap the adzuki paste for Nutella, pistachio butter, or your favorite dessert spread. Also, try topping them with Vanilla Sesame Glaze (page 11) for an ultra-fragrant, mildly sweet finish.

Muffin Base

In my kitchen, muffins came first, and this recipe offers you a beautiful blank canvas to try out your favorite flavors. People often ask about the difference between muffins and cupcakes, and the answer is that cupcakes are muffins in drag. Joking aside, it comes down to density and sugar content. Muffins run denser and less sweet than most cupcakes. Plus, muffins usually don't have frosting . . . which means they're healthy, right?

PREP TIME: 15 minutes
COOK TIME: 25 minutes, plus cooling time
TOTAL TIME: 50 minutes
MAKES: 12 muffins
OCCASIONS: breakfast, post-workout, picnics, hiking, road trips

Neutral nonstick cooking spray (optional)

225 grams (1½ cups) all-purpose flour

½ teaspoon baking soda

½ teaspoon baking powder

½ teaspoon nutmeg

115 grams (½ cup) salted butter, room temperature

200 grams (1 cup) granulated white sugar

2 large eggs, room temperature

120 grams (½ cup) full-fat sour cream or yogurt of choice

1½ teaspoons vanilla extract

55 grams (¼ cup) raw, turbinado, or Demerara sugar (optional)

TIP: Use this recipe exactly as is to make baked donuts in donut-shaped pans. Don't overfill the donut cavity, though, or the batter will expand too much and close the hole.

1   Preheat the oven to 375°F (190°C) and spray a 12-count muffin tin with cooking spray or line the cavities with cupcake liners.

2   In a large bowl, sift together the flour, baking soda, baking powder, and nutmeg.

3   In the bowl of a stand mixer fitted with the paddle attachment or using a hand mixer in a medium mixing bowl, beat the butter on high until smooth and creamy, about 1 minute.

4   Add the sugar and beat on high until the mixture becomes light and fluffy, about 2 minutes. Scrape down the sides and bottom of the bowl as needed.

5   Add the eggs, sour cream, and vanilla extract, beat on medium for 1 minute, then increase the speed to high until the mixture has combined fully. Scrape down the sides and bottom of the bowl at least once to incorporate everything completely.

6   Add the dry ingredients to the wet and mix on low until the batter just combines. For more control, use a spatula and mix by hand.

7   If using any mix-ins, such as dried fruit, frozen fruit, nuts, or chocolate chips, fold them in now.

8   Divide the batter equally among the muffin tin cavities. It's OK if they fill close to the top.

9   If you want your muffin tops to have a nice crunchy crust, sprinkle 1 teaspoon of raw, turbinado, or Demerara sugar on each one.

10   Bake until a toothpick inserted in the center comes out clean, 22 to 25 minutes.

11   Let the muffins cool for 5 minutes in the muffin pan, then transfer to a cooling rack to cool to room temperature.

(recipe continues)

NOTES

In step 6, don't overmix the batter, or the muffins will come out tough.

In step 7, the more modifiers you add, the more batter you'll create, so you might wind up with more than 12 muffins.

For good balance, try not to add more than 1 cup of mix-ins.

In an airtight container or plastic storage bag, the muffins will stay fresh in the fridge for 3 days, or you can freeze them for 3 months.

Thaw frozen muffins at room temperature for 3 to 4 hours before serving or speed the process by microwaving them for 1 minute 30 seconds to 2 minutes on 50 percent power.

VARIATIONS

Try swapping the vanilla extract for vanilla bean paste or powder for beautiful specks.

To make them mini, bake at 350°F (177°C) for 12 to 14 minutes and adjust if using frozen fruit. This recipe yields 24 mini muffins with no mix-ins.

Experiment with flavors. For Lemon Blueberry Muffins (pictured), omit the nutmeg. Add zest from 1 lemon and approximately 1 cup of blueberries, fresh or frozen, in step 7. If using frozen blueberries, your batter will feel cold and ultra-thick, which is OK! For Lychee Muffins, omit the nutmeg. Drain half a 20-ounce (565 grams) can of lychees, reserving the unused juice for Lychee Buttercream (page 38). Rough-chop the fruit and add it in step 7. For Coconut Ube Muffins, omit the nutmeg, replace the vanilla extract with 1½ teaspoons of ube extract, and add 1 cup of toasted coconut flakes in step 7. Top the batter with more toasted coconut flakes before baking. For Five-Spice Crumble Muffins, make the base as is. Before step 8, scoop out approximately 1 cup of batter, stir 1 teaspoon of Chinese five-spice powder into it, and roughly swirl the seasoned batter into the rest. Top with Five-Spice Crumble Topping (page 11) prior to baking.

Five-Spice Crumble Topping

This topping comes from cinnamon swirl coffee cake, but works great for any cake, cupcake, or muffin. Try it on the Muffin Base (page 8), Five-Spice Cookie Bars (page 108), or other cookies iced with buttercream or cream cheese frosting.

PREP TIME: 5 minutes
COOK TIME: 2 minutes
TOTAL TIME: 7 minutes
MAKES: topping for 12 muffins

60 grams (¼ cup) salted butter

65 grams (⅓ packed cup) dark brown sugar

75 grams (½ cup) all-purpose flour

1 teaspoon Chinese five-spice powder

½ teaspoon vanilla extract

1   In a medium, microwave-safe bowl, melt the butter by microwaving it on high for approximately 30 seconds.

2   With a fork, gently stir in the remaining ingredients.

TIP: Don't overmix. You want large crumbles, not a thick paste.

Vanilla Sesame Glaze

This glaze, with its rich nutty flavor and distinct aroma, pairs perfectly with cakes and muffins. Try it on the Muffin Base (page 8) or on sugar cookies or sponge cakes.

PREP TIME: 5 minutes
COOK TIME: 2 minutes
TOTAL TIME: 7 minutes
MAKES: glaze for 12 cupcakes or 1 cake loaf

65 grams (½ cup) toasted white sesame seeds

120 grams (1 cup) confectioners' sugar

45 grams (3 tablespoons) milk or heavy cream

½ teaspoon vanilla extract

1   Toast the sesame seeds for 3 minutes over medium heat until fragrant, keeping the seeds moving to prevent burning. Even though we're using toasted sesame already, it'll add a stronger aroma.

2   In a small bowl, sift the sugar. Add the remaining ingredients and whisk until smooth.

NOTE

Instead of milk or heavy cream, water can work in a pinch. But you'll achieve a thicker glaze with heavy cream or by adding more confectioners' sugar, 1 teaspoon at a time, until you get the desired consistency.

Jiggly Japanese Cheesecake

Many restaurant chains in Japan make these soft, pillowy cakes with the most satisfying jiggle. For good reason, this style of cheesecake is becoming more popular in the USA. Japanese and American cheesecakes both contain cream cheese as a main ingredient, but they have wildly different textures and appearances. Think of it like this: chiffon cake + angel food cake + cheesecake = Japanese cheesecake. Asian desserts tend to taste significantly less sweet than Western ones, which makes this recipe a perfect blank canvas for berries, butters, frostings, jams, and more. Serve with Matcha Coconut Milk Spread (page 130), fresh fruit and confectioners' sugar, berries and fresh whipped cream, or toppings of choice.

PREP TIME: 20 minutes
COOK TIME: 50 minutes
TOTAL TIME: 1 hour 10 minutes
SERVES: 8
OCCASIONS: birthdays, Easter, Thanksgiving, Christmas, bridal showers, baby showers

---

3 eggs, cold

Neutral nonstick cooking spray or butter for greasing

65 grams (⅓ cup) granulated white sugar

120 grams (½ cup) cream cheese

15 grams (1 tablespoon) cornstarch

25 grams (2½ tablespoons) all-purpose flour

60 grams (¼ cup) whole milk

½ teaspoon vanilla extract

¼ teaspoon cream of tartar

1 In a kettle, boil 6 cups of water.

2 While the water is heating, separate the egg whites and yolks.

3 Fill an oven-safe pan, 8 by 8 inches and at least 2 or 3 inches deep, a little more than halfway with the boiling water.

4 Preheat the oven to 330°F (165°C). Place the water bath pan in the oven while you make the cake batter.

5 Coat the bottom of a 6-inch cake pan with cooking spray and then line it with parchment paper. Spray the sides of the pan generously with more cooking spray or grease the sides with butter.

6 In a small pan over medium heat, melt half of the sugar and the cream cheese, stirring constantly, for about 5 minutes. Make sure the mixture incorporates well, becomes smooth, and doesn't burn.

7 Remove from heat and let the mixture cool for 10 minutes.

8 One at a time, whisk in the egg yolks slowly, making sure that you don't make scrambled eggs.

9 Sift in the cornstarch and flour and stir to combine to a smooth batter.

10 Stir in the milk and vanilla and mix to combine. Set aside.

11 Next, prepare the meringue. In the bowl of a stand mixer fitted with a whisk attachment or using a hand mixer in a medium mixing bowl, whisk the egg whites, the remaining half of the sugar, and

(recipe continues)

NOTES

Properly prepping the pan in step 5 ensures that the cheesecake releases after baking.

In an airtight container, it will stay fresh for 1 week in the fridge and for 2 months in the freezer.

It has a higher water content than American-style cheesecake, so don't serve it frozen since it'll be hard as a rock.

the cream of tartar on high speed until stiff peaks form, about 2 minutes 30 seconds to 3 minutes. Do not over beat. If the meringue clumps up inside the whisk and starts to look dry, you'll have to start over.

12   Carefully fold one-third of the meringue into the yolk mixture. You want to combine it well but not deflate the meringue too much.

13   Repeat twice more with the remaining meringue.

14   Pour the batter into the prepared cake pan and tap the pan on the counter a few times to pop any air bubbles. You also can drag a butter knife through the batter to pop bubbles.

15   Carefully remove the water bath pan from the oven, place the cake pan into the oven, and bake for 25 minutes.

16   The cake should have risen and started to brown on top. Reduce the temperature to 250°F (121°C) and bake for 25 more minutes.

17   Turn off the oven and let the cheesecake rest inside it for 10 minutes. The cheesecake should have a brown top, and the sides should have pulled away a bit from the cake pan. As it cools, the cheesecake will continue to shrink a little.

18   Place a serving plate or cake stand upside down over the pan and flip it over to release the cheesecake, which will bounce and jiggle while warm.

19   Enjoy warm or let cool to room temperature and chill in the refrigerator.

TIPS: In step 12, overmixing will result in the cake not rising properly, but undermixing will create a streaky cake with a dense bottom and spongy top layer. You want a light, fluffy, homogenous, pancake-like batter.

During baking, don't open the oven door *at all,* which could cause the cake to collapse.

If, after baking, the top of the cheesecake cracks, your oven might be running hotter than indicated. Next time, try lowering the temperature by 10°F (5.5°C).

The cheesecake wiggles less when cool, so if you want to record those satisfying jiggles, do that right after removing it from the oven and plating it.

Persimmon Pecan Biscotti

In Italian, *biscotti* means cookies. Traditional biscotti don't contain butter and usually bake until hard so they soften when dunked in coffee. That hardness makes them challenging to eat on their own. This recipe uses a little butter to tame the crunch so you can enjoy them without liquid assistance. My ex-sister-in-law once made biscotti with anise extract, which tasted so interesting. With the right amount, you'll achieve good depth of flavor without conjuring a mouthful of licorice.

PREP TIME: 15 minutes
COOK TIME: 40 minutes, plus cooling time
TOTAL TIME: 1 hour 15 minutes
MAKES: 12 large biscotti
OCCASIONS: Thanksgiving, Christmas, bake sales, and picnics

---

90 grams (¾ cup) toasted pecans

50 grams (¼ cup) dried persimmons

60 grams (¼ cup) salted butter, room temperature

150 grams (¾ cup) granulated white sugar

2 large eggs, room temperature

1 teaspoon baking soda

1 teaspoon vanilla extract

⅓ teaspoon anise extract

300 grams (2 cups) all-purpose flour

NOTES

At the end of the second bake, it's OK if the cookies don't feel solid. They'll harden as they cool. Store them in an airtight container on the counter for up to 3 weeks or in the freezer for up to 5 months.

1 Preheat the oven to 350°F (177°C), roughly chop the nuts and fruit, and line a baking sheet with parchment paper or a silicone baking mat.

2 In the bowl of a stand mixer fitted with the flat beater attachment, cream the butter and sugar on medium until fluffy, about 2 minutes.

3 One at a time, add the eggs and continue beating to incorporate.

4 Add the baking soda, vanilla extract, and anise extract and continue beating for a few seconds to combine.

5 All at once, add the flour and chopped nuts and fruit and mix on low until just combined and the dough pulls away naturally from the edge of the bowl, about 1 minute 30 seconds.

6 Turn the dough out onto the prepared baking sheet and form it into a 14-by-5-by-1-inch rectangle.

7 Bake for 25 minutes, rotating halfway through.

8 Remove the biscotti block from the oven, keeping the oven on, and let the block cool for 20 minutes.

9 Transfer the block to a cutting board and use a bread or other serrated knife to slice the block into logs.

10 Return the biscotti to the baking sheet, leaving space among them, and bake for 15 more minutes.

11 Remove from the oven, turn it off, and let the biscotti cool to room temperature before serving.

Persimmon
Pecan Biscotti

VARIATIONS

For Almond Mango Biscotti, use slivered almonds and dried mango chunks. Have fun customizing this recipe. Use any dried fruits and nuts of your choice, such as apricots, cranberries, pistachios, hazelnuts, walnuts, and so forth.

Mini Triple-Chocolate
Cheesecakes

Mini Triple-Chocolate Cheesecakes

In college, my ex-husband and I went on dates to The Cheesecake Factory and always brought home a slice of Godiva Chocolate Cheesecake. This dessert pays homage to that indulgence. Cupcake-size cheesecakes make so much sense. Mini foods look cute, smaller portion sizes can trick the mind into (a little) self-control, and cupcake liners mean fewer dishes to clean. What's not to love? Before I started baking, I assumed that cheesecake was difficult to make, which couldn't have been further from the truth! A true artisan cheesecake requires serious commitment and expertise, yes, but this easy chocolate-lover's recipe requires significantly less time and will take you 90 percent of the way there. Serve with whipped cream and toppings of choice, such as berries or, you guessed it, more chocolate.

PREP TIME: 25 minutes
COOK TIME: 25 minutes, plus resting and cooling time
TOTAL TIME: 8 hours
MAKES: 12 mini cheesecakes
OCCASIONS: dinner parties, birthdays, anniversaries, Valentine's Day, Mother's Day, Christmas

FOR THE CRUST

10 chocolate sandwich cookies

45 grams (3 tablespoons) butter of choice

FOR THE CHEESECAKE

115 grams (⅔ cup) semi-sweet chocolate chips

55 grams (¼ cup) hot coffee

227 grams (8 ounces) cream cheese, room temperature

135 grams (⅔ cup) granulated white sugar

30 grams (2 tablespoons) sour cream, room temperature

1 teaspoon vanilla extract

1 egg, room temperature

10 grams (1 tablespoon) all-purpose flour

1   Preheat the oven to 325°F (163°C) and line a muffin tin with 12 paper cupcake liners.

2   For the crust: In a food processor, pulse the whole cookies into crumbs. If you don't have a food processor, put the cookies in a plastic storage bag and, with the bottom of a heavy mug, pan, or rolling pin, smash them into crumbs.

3   Melt the butter in the microwave and stir it into the cookie crumbs.

4   Divide the crumb mixture equally into the cupcake liners. With a muddler or the bottom of a Collins or other tall, thin glass, press firmly to pack the crust tightly.

5   For the cheesecake: In a small bowl, add the chocolate chips and pour the hot coffee over them. Stir the mixture a few times and microwave it on high in 10-second intervals as needed, stirring between each interval, until all the chunks have melted.

6   In the bowl of a stand mixer fitted with a paddle attachment or using a hand mixer in a medium mixing bowl, beat the cream cheese on medium until smooth, 1 minute 30 seconds to 2 minutes.

7   Add the sugar and continue beating until well combined, about 1 minute.

8   Scrape down the sides of the bowl, add the sour cream and vanilla extract, and continue beating to combine for 1 more minute.

FOR THE GANACHE

55 grams (⅓ cup) chocolate chips

60 grams (2 ounces) heavy whipping cream

15 grams (1 tablespoon) cold salted butter

TIP: For toppings, add your favorite chocolate candy. Twix or Kit Kats add a nice crunch.

NOTES

If, when baking, the cheesecakes crack, remove them from the oven—they're done! Casual cheesecake lovers won't mind a few cracks, and if you cover them with ganache, no one will know. The cheesecakes should puff a bit and not deflate much after baking.

They stay fresh in the fridge for 5 days, and you can freeze them for 3 months. They taste great straight from the freezer, like firm ice cream, but you can defrost them in the fridge overnight to restore their soft, smooth, creamy texture.

9   Add the egg, sift the flour into the bowl, and continue beating to combine until smooth and creamy, 1 minute 30 seconds to 2 minutes.

10   Add the chocolate-coffee mixture and stir with a spatula until the batter becomes homogenous.

11   Divide the batter equally among the 12 cupcake liners.

12   Bake until the centers dome and crack a little, 22 to 25 minutes, rotating halfway through.

13   In the tin, let the cheesecakes cool for 20 to 30 minutes.

14   While the cheesecakes are cooling, make the ganache. Add the chocolate chips to a small bowl.

15   In a microwave-safe measuring cup, microwave the cream on high until it begins to boil, 45 seconds to 1 minute. Watch the cream closely to make sure it doesn't boil over.

16   Pour the hot cream over the chocolate chips, let it stand for 5 minutes, then stir. If chocolate chunks remain, microwave the chocolate cream on high in 10-second intervals as needed, stirring between each interval, until the mixture becomes smooth.

17   Stir in the cold butter, which will melt uniformly.

18   Pour the ganache over the cooled cheesecakes and chill them in the refrigerator overnight.

VARIATIONS

Instead of crushing the sandwich cookies into a crust, you can use a whole cookie as the base and build the mini cheesecake on it.

Instead of brewed coffee, you can substitute 1 teaspoon of instant coffee or espresso in 55 grams (¼ cup) hot water or, if you want to get fancy, use 1 shot of espresso with enough hot water added to make 55 grams (¼ cup) of liquid.

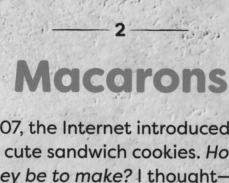

2

Macarons

In 2007, the Internet introduced me to these cute sandwich cookies. *How hard can they be to make?* I thought—naively. The Internet didn't tell me how difficult they can be. But I want you to learn from my experience because making them successfully makes them taste even better.

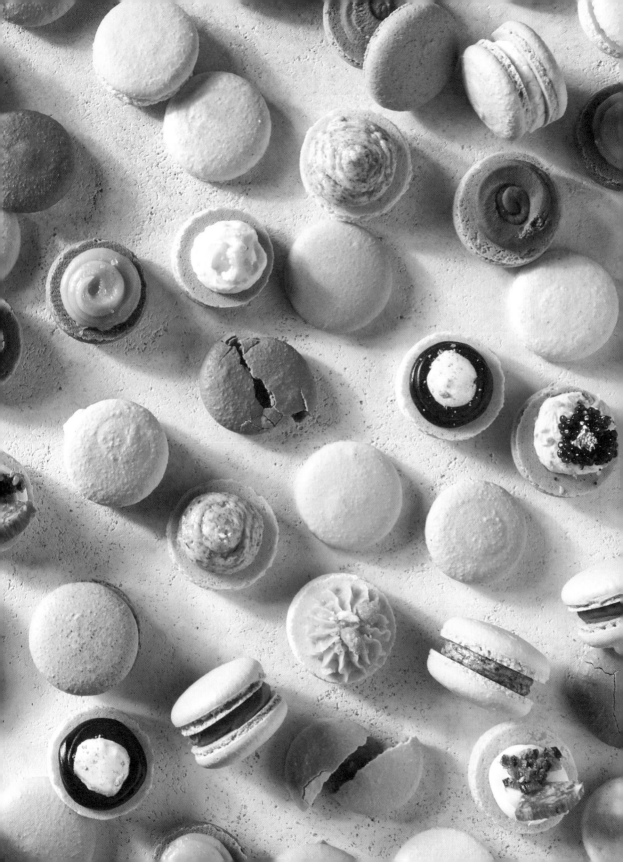

A SHORT INTRODUCTION TO MACARONS

These almond-based meringue cookies, my first love, have smooth shells and small bubbles or ruffles at the bottom adorably called feet. The crisp, somewhat fragile shells resemble confectionery eggshells that, when broken apart, reveal a fluffy, chewy cookie inside. Little pockets of filling, such as buttercream, ganache, or jam, join two shells to create the tasty indulgence. You need minimal equipment to make them: not many bowls, no boiling sugar, pretty easy cleanup. They also freeze well, making them a great treat to prep in advance. Macarons don't take much time to make, but learning how to make them properly can take a while. Let's not be maca-snobs, though. Everyone who has made them runs into at least a few maca-wrongs, and that's OK. It's part of the learning process. This chapter provides my tried-and-true shell recipe, along with a handful of filling recipes and my approach to flavorings. Hopefully, it will encourage you to create your own taste bud–tickling flavors. Macarons don't work for people with nut allergies, but keep reading for a handy substitution. Save your yolks and check out the Recipes for Extra Yolks (page 51) for good ways to use them.

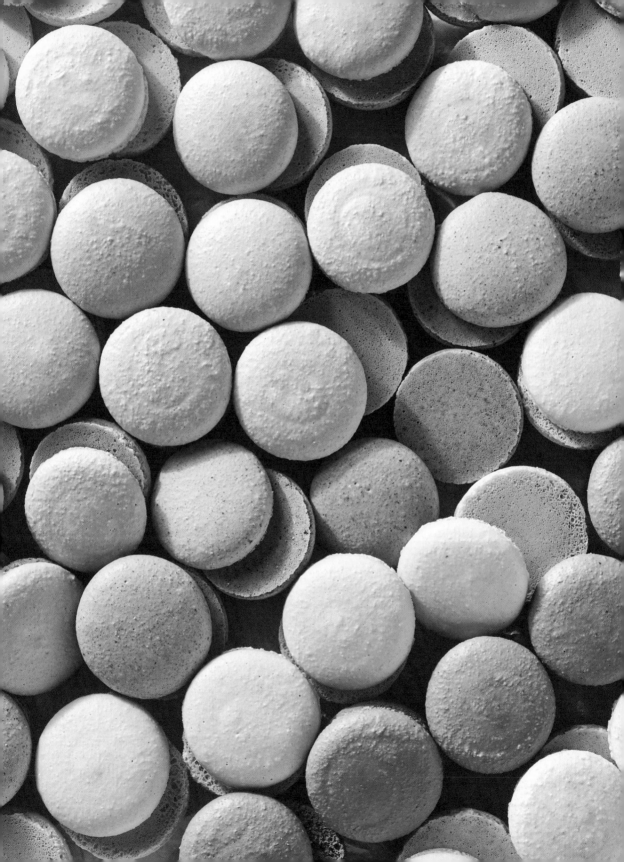

Macaron Shells

When starting your macaron journey, you need to get your shell recipe down with no modifications. Only when you consistently make great shells can you experiment with colors, different nuts, powder flavors, pulverized cereal, and other variations. So follow the instructions in this chapter carefully.

Macaron Shells

Traditional macaron shells have a lightly chewy, fluffy interior and taste quite sweet. This recipe has a slightly more robust exterior, a firmer inside, and tastes less sweet.

PREP TIME: 15 minutes
COOK TIME: 16 minutes, plus resting and cooling time
TOTAL TIME: 1 hour
MAKES: 32 shells (1½-inch diameter)

---

65 grams (¼ cup) egg whites, from 2 large eggs

65 grams (⅓ cup) granulated white sugar

80 grams (¾ cup) almond flour, finely ground or superfine

75 grams (½ cup) confectioners' sugar

TIPS: When separating the eggs, try to keep the yolks intact. In step 7, err on the side of under-mixing rather than overmixing.

1   First, make the meringue base. Into the bowl of a stand mixer, add the egg whites. Reserve yolks for other use (page 51).

2   Add the sugar, fit the whisk attachment to the mixer, and whisk on low until the mixture froths with big bubbles at first and tighter, whiter bubbles as it progresses, about 2 minutes.

3   While the meringue is whipping, sift together the almond flour and confectioners' sugar. Set aside.

4   Increase the mixer speed to medium and whip until the small bubbles become a shiny white meringue, about 5 more minutes.

5   While the meringue continues whipping, fit a large piping bag with a round, ¼-inch diameter tip (#12) and prep your cookie sheet. For this recipe, silicone baking mats on aluminum cookie sheets work well. If desired, slide a piping template under the mat to help with piping consistent shells.

6   Increase the mixer speed to the highest setting and whip the meringue until it becomes glossy, about 4 more minutes. It should resemble shaving cream rather than whipped cream. The meringue should clump in the whisk but not look broken or dry. If using food coloring, add it now.

7   Add the dry mixture to the meringue and, with a rubber or silicone spatula, fold it until the mixture resembles flowing lava. This process is called macaronage (see Tips).

8   Transfer the mixture to the prepared piping bag.

9   Onto the silicone baking mat, pipe your macarons into 1½-inch-diameter circles. Keep your piping tip perpendicular to the baking mat and squeeze, allowing the batter to pool around the piping tip. Release pressure gradually and twirl to stop the flow of batter.

(recipe continues)

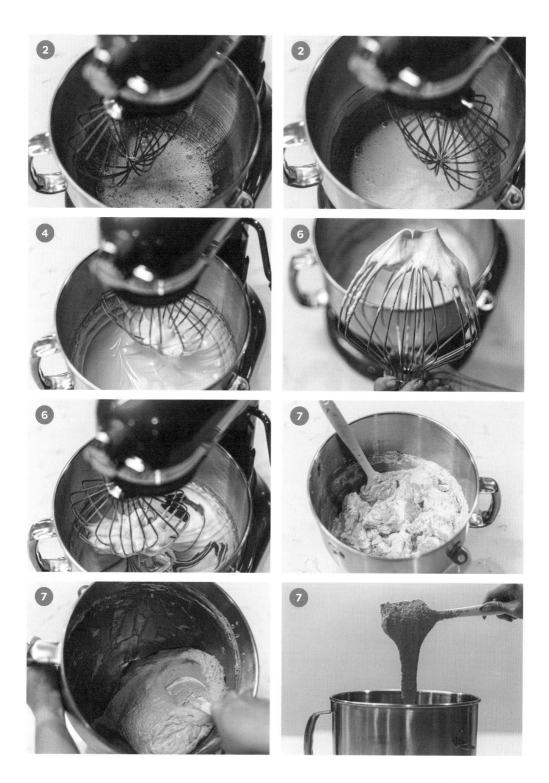

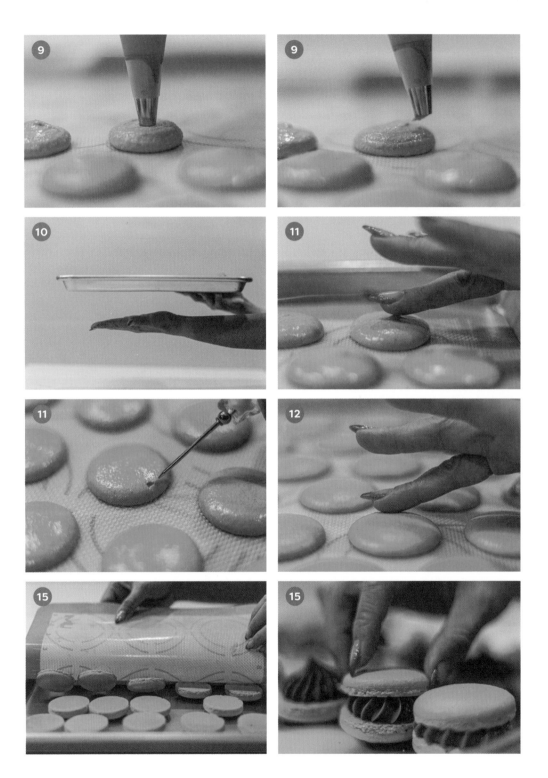

10   Firmly tap the bottoms of the cookie sheets to settle the batter and release air bubbles.

11   With a slightly wet finger, gently smooth any nipples in the batter and use a toothpick or cookie scribe to pop any remaining air bubbles and to maneuver the batter if necessary.

12   Preheat the oven to 300°F (150°C) and let the raw shells rest for 20 minutes to form a skin.

13   Bake for 16 minutes, rotating halfway through. The macarons are done baking if, when you gently nudge a shell with your finger, it barely moves. If cooked completely and cooled properly, they should pop cleanly and easily from the baking mat. The bottoms should look smooth and even, leaving little to no residue behind.

14   Remove the macarons from the oven and let them cool completely on the trays, about 30 minutes.

15   Remove the macarons from the baking mats, pair them by size, and fill.

VARIATION

For those with nut allergies, substitute the almond flour with the same weight of unsalted, roasted pumpkin seeds. In a blender or food processor, pulse the seeds with the confectioners' sugar to a fine powder, about 2 minutes. Filter through a sieve before using.

NOTES

Don't use liquid egg whites from a carton. The pasteurization process weakens the proteins and makes it difficult to achieve a stable meringue. Don't let the eggs warm to room temperature. Separate the whites straight from the fridge.

When adding color and other modifications, bake time may change. For example, using a lot of gel color will create more moisture in the batter, so it will need a few more minutes to cook. Length of rest time will vary depending on environment. The more humid, the longer you'll need to wait. In a high-humidity climate, you may have to rest your shell batter for up to 2 hours. When the shell batter forms a skin, you want to be able to touch the side of the raw shell gently without any wet batter transferring to your finger.

If you used a piping template, don't forget to remove it from the cookie sheet before baking!

In an airtight container, filled macarons will stay moist in the fridge for about 1 week and in the freezer will stay fresh for about 3 months. But those numbers depend on the filling and how much moisture it contains.

ADVANCED MACARON SHELL SHAPES

After you've mastered basic shells, you can pipe them in lots of different ways to create shapes such as rosettes, florals, characters, and other designs.

For rosettes, undermix your batter a little, making sure that it still holds its shape, and use a 1M tip. The accompanying pictures will help guide you.

For flower petals, use a 104 tip.

When piping characters or other intricate designs, pipe alternative sections and let them crust for about 10 minutes between each section. This technique allows you to see the separations between sections. Pipe as much batter as you can so the macarons don't end up flat, with teeny feet.

To create different colors from one batch of batter, roughly mix the dry ingredients into the meringue so that it just combines. Portion the batter into however many colors you want and finish the macaronage process for each color separately.

MACARON SHELL FLAVORS

As much as possible, stick to the recipe for Macaron Shells (page 26). Use food coloring to imply flavor, but don't go crazy with these modifications until you can create reliable results. When eating a macaron, you bite the whole thing, shell and filling, so use the fillings to generate most of the flavor. Keeping the shells as plain as possible reduces the risk of flubbing their chemistry. Liquid extracts and flavorings that contain fat can weaken the meringue. Almond flour already contains some fat, so limit adding more. With that in mind, try these flavor modifications for your shells.

CHOCOLATE: Substitute no more than 5 percent of the almond flour, by weight, with sifted cocoa powder. Use brown food coloring to achieve the desired shade of brown.

COOKIES 'N' CREAM: Substitute no more than 10 percent of the almond flour, by weight, with superfine cookies 'n' cream crumbs or pulverized sandwich cookies, which will result in pretty, speckled shells.

FRUITY CEREAL: Substitute no more than 10 percent of the almond flour, by weight, with superfine cereal crumbs or pulverized cereal.

S'MORES: Substitute no more than 10 percent of the almond flour, by weight, with superfine graham cracker crumbs or pulverized graham crackers.

STRAWBERRY: Substitute no more than 5 percent of the almond flour, by weight, with pulverized freeze-dried strawberries. Use a tiny bit of red food coloring to achieve the desired shade of pink.

Troubleshooting Macaron Shells

Macarons require a lot of technique and self-awareness. The process involves so many parameters—environment, equipment, technique—that only you can figure out what went wrong and how to fix it. The chemistry of cooking depends not only on ingredients but also on elevation, temperature, humidity, order of operations, and so on. Troubleshoot by tracking everything you do, then change *one* parameter at a time and document your results so you can review what changes had what impact. It takes time and effort, but it's worth the results. Use this overview of the most common problems with macarons to help you troubleshoot.

Hollow Macarons

For completely full shells, you must achieve the perfect balance of proper technique plus ideal baking temperature and time. Again—and I can't stress this enough—achieving that balance comes with awareness, repetition, and experimentation. Not all hollows are the same, and a range of factors can result in different kinds of hollows.

- Underbeating the meringue can cause hollows, as can overmixing the batter. In both cases, the problem lies with the meringue, which is finicky. Once it breaks, you can't fix it.

- If the batter sits in the piping bag too long, more than 15 to 20 minutes, it will start to break down.

- Baking. Mats. Matter. Every brand of baking mat and baking sheet conducts heat differently. Some people achieve fuller shells by using parchment paper over the silicone mats, but that result also depends on how heat moves in your oven.

- Oven temperature can cause hollows in two ways. Too high and the batter sets before it can rise. Too low—almost a hollow guarantee—and the batter can't rise. If (you think that) your oven isn't stable, heat a pizza stone on the lowest rack for 1 hour before baking to help stabilize the appliance's temperature.

- Underbaking, even if by only a few minutes, can cause hollows. During the bake, the inside batter bubbles up and adheres inside the top of the shell. If underbaked, the insides won't stick to the top and will collapse as the shell cools.

Half Hollow with Tall Feet

Overbeating the meringue usually causes this result. You likely passed the "shaving cream" consistency, and the meringue probably started to break into large, dry-looking chunks. You can't save meringue beaten to this level of submission.

Hollows around Center of Shells

In most cases, this problem gets a pass. But if you're exacting, this symptom usually results from undermixed batter. In such cases, not enough air folded out of the batter and giant bubbles remained. Proper macaronage breaks most of the air bubbles, resulting in homogenous batter. Undermixed batter keeps its shape *too* well after piping and barely spreads. After baking, undermixed shells tend to have a harder, thicker outer layer. But there's a silver lining! The beauty of undermixed macarons is that, after filling and maturing, the shells absorb moisture from the filling and the texture improves. Most people won't be able to tell that it's undermixed.

Minor Gaps at Top of Shells

Not a big deal, especially since most gaps resolve on their own after Maturation (page 37), but it still presents a good learning opportunity. Macarons with minor gaps at the top tend to have more of a dome shape. A few more taps on the bottom of the baking sheet can help the batter spread a bit more and eliminate the gaps.

Fragile, Thin, "Oily" Shells That Break Easily

This situation likely results from overmixed batter *or* underbeaten meringue or maybe a combination of the two. If you've ruled out both those possibilities, examine your almond flour, which can become oily when refrigerated or from sitting around for a long time. Additional fat also can create fragile shells. Cocoa powder, matcha, and other shell modifications that contain oils can cause this problem.

Cracked Shells

These result when too much heat is applied to quickly, or when the raw shells didn't rest enough to form a film before baking.

Feet Spread Outward

If this is the only problem and everything else looks as it should, your oven may be running too hot. Try reducing the temperature by 5°F (2.7°C). If spread feet accompany hollow or fragile shells, the meringue broke either from underbeating or overbeating.

No Feet or Teeny Feet

This problem can result for several reasons that depend on other simultaneous symptoms. Tapping the bottom of the tray too much sometimes causes too much spread, resulting in no feet. Not resting the shells long enough can cause tiny feet. Oven temperature also could be running a bit low.

Color Woes

Food coloring has come a long way, and it's easier than ever to achieve vibrant or dark colors. Both powders and gels work for coloring macarons, but gel affects the batter. If you're going for something dark or vibrant with a gel, bake the macarons for a few more minutes. If you don't, the shells will stick to the mat and leave macaron guts when you try to remove them. Vibrant or deep colors such as red, navy blue, or black require a *lot* of gel color, so, to avoid introducing additional moisture, use powders (page 75).

WHAT TO DO WITH MACA-WRONGS

When making macarons, everyone encounters maca-wrongs. It's absolutely normal and part of the process. Angry and frustrated, I have tossed *countless* batches. But no more because now I know better, so I do better. Consider doing the same.

- Crumble imperfect shells for an ice cream topping or smash them together for a crust for your next cheesecake, pie, or tart.

- Make it cake. Alternate broken shells with buttercream or whipped cream and top with fruit.

- Mix crumbled shells with a little buttercream and form into balls or other shapes. Dip in chocolate or a coating of choice to make gluten-free "cake" pops or truffles.

- Macaron de Jayne, a Bay Area bakery, invented tira-mac-su by using busted macaron shells instead of ladyfingers. Genius! Experiment with different jams and flavored buttercreams to create different flavors.

Sweet Macaron Fillings

Macaron shells look and function like hamburger buns: fine on their own, but the filling completes them. Keeping the shells simple leaves less room for error and allows you to lean into fillings for flavor. The filling recipes in this section come with recommendations for different flavor modifications. Depending on the recipe and how you modify it, the moisture content will vary, which will affect texture. But, again, a silver lining! If you overbaked your shells, compensate by making a moister filling, which will permeate the shell as the macaron matures.

Maturation

Macarons taste best after they mature. Maturation means the process in which shells and filling meld, with the overall texture becoming more consistent and chewier throughout the cookie. The moisture from the filling enters the shell, helping the insides of the shells relax and fluff a bit more. Maturation helps flavor and texture develop fully, and it usually fixes maca-wrongs, such as small gaps between the top of the shells and the insides, some air pockets, and slightly crunchy shells. As moisture permeates the shell, it also reduces the chances of filling squeezing out the sides. When you bite into a macaron, the filling should stay put. Mature your finished macarons overnight in an airtight container so they don't dry out.

Lychee Buttercream Filling

In China, lychees are as common as apples in America. They're becoming more popular here, but they weren't easy to obtain in San Francisco in the 1990s. One year, my mom found some at the grocery store, and she, Dad, Grandma, and I sat around the table to enjoy them together, all of us delighted. If you haven't had them, they're small fruits about the size of a walnut, with a strong, bumpy red skin and translucent, sweet flesh that has a slightly floral aroma.

The texture feels like firm jelly, and the flavor combines notes of strawberry, pear, and grape. Don't eat the pits. Growers usually harvest them between May and July, but you can buy them year-round in a can, which is totally OK! Canned lychees taste great, don't have pits, and come in a syrup that's perfect for making this recipe.

PREP TIME: 5 minutes

TOTAL TIME: 10 minutes

MAKES: filling for 36 macarons (1½-inch diameter)

OCCASIONS: Chinese New Year, Easter

---

225 grams (1 cup) salted butter, room temperature

One 20-ounce (566-gram) can lychees (we're using just 7 or 8 lychees; reserve the syrup)

400 grams (2⅔ cups) confectioners' sugar

¼ teaspoon almond extract

1 In the bowl of a stand mixer fitted with the paddle attachment, beat the butter on medium speed until fluffy, about 2 minutes.

2 While the butter is beating, drain and finely dice 7 or 8 lychees from the can. Set aside.

3 Into the bowl of butter, add the confectioners' sugar, 3 tablespoons of syrup from the can of lychees, and the almond extract and beat to combine.

4 Fold the diced lychees into the buttercream.

5 Transfer to a piping bag and use immediately or freeze for up to 3 months.

TIP: If freezing or refrigerating this filling, for best results always bring it to room temperature before piping.

Cream Cheese Filling

This recipe makes a stable, not-too-sweet filling that also works great for frosting cakes and cookies.

PREP TIME: 5 minutes

TOTAL TIME: 10 minutes

MAKES: approximately 4 cups of frosting

OCCASIONS: birthdays, dinner parties, Valentine's Day, St. Patrick's Day, Easter, Derby Day, Independence Day, Halloween, Thanksgiving

225 grams (1½ cups) confectioners' sugar

170 grams (¾ cup) salted butter, room temperature

454 grams (two 8-ounce blocks) full-fat Philadelphia cream cheese, cold

1 teaspoon vanilla extract

VARIATIONS

For cookies 'n' cream, fold pulverized cookie crumbs into the frosting after the last step. For strawberry cheesecake, add pulverized graham crackers and pulverized freeze-dried strawberries after the last step. Allow these modified fillings to rest in the refrigerator for 3 hours for the flavors to combine.

1   Sift the confectioners' sugar.

2   In the bowl of a stand mixer fitted with the paddle attachment, cream the butter and confectioners' sugar until the butter becomes light and fluffy, about 3 minutes. Start on low speed and move gradually to medium.

3   Add the cream cheese all at once and continue beating on medium until you achieve a thick, smooth frosting, about 2 minutes. Don't overmix.

4   Add the vanilla extract and beat just to combine.

NOTES

The Philadelphia brand works best for this recipe because its full-fat cream cheese has the best texture and flavor and the lowest water content.

Cream cheese sometimes can split or become "wet" from overworking, which releases water from the mixture. Not overbeating and combining ingredients in the specified order will result in a more stable filling.

The filling will stay fresh in the fridge for 5 days and will keep in the freezer for 2 months.

Miso Caramel Filling

If you like sweet and salty, this filling is for you. Miso adds savory depth to the buttery caramel. Some brands of miso paste can run quite salty, so experiment to find the right one for the flavor profile that you want.

PREP TIME: 5 minutes

COOK TIME: 15 minutes, plus cooling time

TOTAL TIME: 1 hour

MAKES: filling for 36 macarons (1½-inch diameter)

OCCASIONS: Valentine's Day, Super Bowl Sunday, Cherry Blossom Festival, Halloween, Thanksgiving

100 grams (½ cup) granulated white sugar

20 grams (1¼ tablespoons) water

80 grams (⅓ cup) heavy cream

45 grams (3 tablespoons) salted butter

15 grams (1 tablespoon) miso paste

½ teaspoon vanilla extract

NOTE

In an airtight container, the filling will stay fresh in the refrigerator for 2 weeks and will keep in the freezer for 3 months.

1 In a medium saucepan over medium-high heat, add the sugar and water and stir occasionally until the sugar dissolves, about 5 minutes.

2 Increase the heat to high and bring the syrup to a boil. Once it starts boiling, don't stir it.

3 Continue cooking until the mixture turns dark amber, 6 to 8 minutes.

4 Remove the pan from the heat and carefully whisk in the heavy cream, then the butter, miso paste, and vanilla extract.

5 Let cool to room temperature.

TIP: In step 3, watch the syrup carefully to ensure that it doesn't burn, which can happen quickly. Slather this filling on apples or glaze them with it and thank me later.

VARIATION

Miso comes in different types: white, yellow, red, and black. The colors mostly indicate how long the soybeans fermented and what other ingredients the paste contains. Flavors range from light and sweeter (white, yellow) to heartier and more flavorful (red, black).

Chocolate Ganache Filling

Use your chocolate of choice, milk or dark, with the same ratios.

PREP TIME: 5 minutes

COOK TIME: 5 minutes, plus cooling time

TOTAL TIME: 3 hours

MAKES: filling for 36 macarons (1½-inch diameter)

OCCASIONS: birthdays, dinner parties, bridal showers, weddings, Valentine's Day, Halloween, Christmas

---

180 grams (⅔ cup) heavy whipping cream

225 grams (1⅛ cups) chocolate chips

15 grams (1 tablespoon) salted butter, cold

TIP: When microwaving the cream, don't let it boil or you'll risk breaking the ganache.

VARIATION

Ganache reaches its final texture after it cools to room temperature. After you make it a few times and understand the target texture, play with the ratios of chocolate to cream to thicken or thin it.

1   In a microwave-safe bowl, microwave the heavy whipping cream and chocolate chips on medium-high (level 7 of 10) for 1 minute.

2   Let it stand for 2 minutes, stir, and repeat for 30-second intervals until the chocolate fully melts.

3   Add the butter and stir until it fully incorporates.

4   Let the ganache set at room temperature for 2 hours before piping.

NOTES

You can store the set ganache in the fridge, but it'll feel very hard. Let it come to room temperature for 2 hours before using. If the ganache isn't setting, consider the following:

• Are you using heavy whipping cream? Not half-and-half, not cream, not light whipping cream, not heavy cream. The container must read HEAVY WHIPPING CREAM.

• Are you using candy melts instead of chocolate chips? Candy melts or almond bark won't work for this recipe.

• Try using chocolate chips with a higher cocoa content.

• Brand of chocolate matters. Try another and see if that makes a difference.

White Chocolate Ganache Filling

This recipe is, hands down, my favorite filling for macarons. Making white chocolate into a ganache tones down its sweetness and creates a blank canvas perfect for adding other flavors. It also pipes beautifully and has a satisfyingly smooth, dense texture. You should use pure white chocolate for this recipe, preferably a bar that you can chop up. Don't use white chocolate chips, which have a special coating that make them hard to melt, or melting chips or vanilla chips, which are not pure white chocolate.

PREP TIME: 5 minutes

COOK TIME: 7 minutes

TOTAL TIME: 3 hours

MAKES: filling for 24 macarons (1½-inch diameter)

OCCASIONS: bridal showers, weddings, baby showers, Valentine's Day, Independence Day, Halloween, Thanksgiving, Christmas, New Year's Eve

120 grams (½ cup) heavy whipping cream

160 grams (1 cup) white chocolate

15 grams (1 tablespoon) salted butter, cold

1 In a microwave-safe bowl, microwave the heavy whipping cream and chocolate on medium-high (level 7 of 10) for 1 minute.

2 Let it stand for 2 minutes, stir, and repeat for 30-second intervals until the chocolate fully melts.

3 Add the butter and stir until it fully incorporates.

4 Let the ganache set at room temperature for 2 hours before piping.

TIPS: When microwaving the cream, don't let it boil or you'll risk breaking the ganache.

If your white chocolate isn't melting, try blending it with a stick blender or countertop appliance to give it some help. (This problem usually happens only with low-quality white chocolate.)

NOTE

You can store the set ganache in the fridge, but it'll feel very hard. Let it come to room temperature for 2 hours before using.

VARIATIONS

Try these flavor modifications.

CEREAL: In a blender or food processer, pulse your favorite cereal to a fine powder and add the desired amount to the ganache. Don't add too much powder, though, or it will harden the chocolate. Start with 35 grams (3 tablespoons) per batch of ganache, taste, test, and adjust if necessary.

COOKIES 'N' CREAM: In a blender or food processor, pulse 6 sandwich cookies of choice to a powder and add crushed sandwich cookies to the ganache.

FRUIT: Add 15 to 30 grams (1 to 2 tablespoons) of jam of choice per batch of ganache. Good choices include apricot, blackberry, fig, guava, lemon, lychee, mango, orange, papaya, passion fruit, peach, pear, plum, raspberry, strawberry, and yuzu. Add ¼ teaspoon of matching extract only if the flavor needs a boost. You can also pipe a ring of this filling and add some straight-up jam into the center.

You also can add pulverized freeze-dried fruit for an interesting twist. The jam-and-freeze-dried-fruit concept extends to all flavors. You may need to adjust the amount of heavy whipping cream, but that depends on the moisture content of the jam and freeze-dried fruit. Experiment and adjust accordingly. If the ganache runs too thin, add more white chocolate; if too thick, add more heavy whipping cream.

MATCHA: Add an additional 15 grams (½ ounce) of heavy whipping cream and 20 grams (1 tablespoon) of sifted matcha. (Matcha is drying, so the filling needs a little more moisture.)

PISTACHIO: Add 1 part pistachio paste to 3 parts filling.

SWEET CORN: Add an additional 30 grams (1 ounce) of heavy whipping cream and 30 grams of sweet corn powder.

UBE: Add 2 teaspoons of ube extract.

Savory Macaron Fillings

If you or your loved ones have less of a sweet tooth, or if you just want to try something different, these savory macaron fillings are for you. These fillings draw inspiration from charcuterie boards assembled from cheeses, meats, nuts, and sweet bites. As the COVID-19 pandemic started, making my own mini grazing boards helped me fill the void when I couldn't socialize physically with others by overloading my taste buds as much as possible. These macarons look good, taste great, and serve perfectly at get-togethers.

Honey Brie Chili Crisp Filling

Until recently, cheese wasn't popular in China, and truth be told: I'm no cheese lover. When I moved to America, the amount of cheese on pizza repelled me. On a business trip to Europe in 2022, coworkers took me to a wine-and-cheese tasting. To save face, I pretended to enjoy cheese. But it turned out that I didn't have to fake it because European styles made me appreciate cheese in a way that American styles couldn't. The flavors were clean, not overly pungent. I returned stateside with my mind open to finding cheese that I enjoyed. Brie has a smooth, super creamy texture, and it pairs so well with sweet and savory foods. One day, I topped a garlic herb biscuit with Brie, honey, and chili crisp oil, which instantly made me want to try it with macarons. So here we are.

PREP TIME: 2 minutes

TOTAL TIME: 5 minutes

MAKES: filling for 24 macarons (1½-inch diameter)

OCCASIONS: dinner parties, girls' night, weddings, baby showers, Super Bowl Sunday, Thanksgiving, New Year's Eve

---

1 Brie wheel, 6-inch diameter

45 grams (2 tablespoons) honey

Chili crisp oil, to taste

Salami (optional)

TIP: To limit the sweetness, leave these macarons open-faced. You can create sandwiches, but they may taste overly sweet.

1 Cut the cheese wheel in half and use a spoon to scoop the cheese from the rind.

2 In a small bowl, add the scooped cheese and, with a rubber or silicone spatula, stir the Brie until smooth.

3 Transfer the cheese to a piping bag and pipe onto macaron shells.

4 Add a drizzle of honey and chili crisp oil and salami, if desired, to taste and serve immediately.

> **NOTES**
>
> Make the shells for this filling with no modifications or flavors. Replace 20 percent of the confectioners' sugar, by weight, with more almond flour. Color them however you like. After piping, consider sprinkling black and white toasted sesame seeds on top.
>
> The filling will stay fresh in the fridge for 1 week or will keep in the freezer for 1 month.

Salted Egg Yolk and Scallion Filling

As a kid, I ate scallion pancakes with salted duck eggs and rice porridge for break-fast all the time. The yolks were my favorite part. Salted chicken egg yolks taste similar, and this recipe combines the flavors of my childhood with the essence of fried cream cheese rangoons found frequently in American Chinese restaurants. This filling also nods to my favorite moon cakes—lotus paste and salted egg yolks—that my family enjoys every year during the Mid-Autumn Festival.

PREP TIME: 5 minutes

TOTAL TIME: 10 minutes

MAKES: filling for 48 macarons (1½-inch diameter)

OCCASIONS: dinner parties, girls' night, bridal showers, Chinese New Year, Mid-Autumn Festival

4 Salted Egg Yolks (page 53)

3 or 4 stalks green onions, white and green parts

227 grams (8 ounces) cream cheese, room temperature

VARIATION

Instead of green onions, try chives.

1 Finely grate the yolks with a microplane and finely chop the green onions.

2 In a stand mixer fitted with the paddle attachment or using a hand mixer in a medium bowl, beat the cream cheese on medium until soft and smooth, about 3 minutes.

3 Stir in the grated yolks and chopped green onions.

4 Transfer to a piping bag, pipe onto macaron shells, top with corresponding shells if desired or leave open-faced, and serve immediately.

NOTES

Make the shells for this filling with no modifications or flavors. Reduce the confectioners' sugar content by 20 percent. Color them however you like. Leave them open-faced or sandwich with another shell.

The filling will stay fresh in the fridge for 1 week or will keep in the freezer for 1 month.

Everything Minus the Bagel with Lox Filling

This recipe plays on an everything bagel with lox. With it you can create an adorable mini appetizer that tastes great.

If you're not sure how you want to use them, the yolks freeze nicely. Add two yolks to a sealable plastic snack bag, seal it, and freeze for later use.

PREP TIME: 5 minutes

TOTAL TIME: 10 minutes

MAKES: filling for 48 macarons (1½-inch diameter)

OCCASIONS: Shabbat, Rosh Hashanah, Hanukkah

---

1 lemon

113 grams (4 ounces) smoked salmon

50 grams (½ cup) scallions, white and green parts

227 grams (8 ounces) cream cheese, room temperature

½ teaspoon fresh dill

½ teaspoon fine sea salt

¼ teaspoon freshly cracked black pepper

15 grams (2 tablespoons) brined capers, drained

1 Zest the lemon and juice it, roughly chop the salmon, and thinly slice the scallions.

2 In a medium mixing bowl, use a fork to stir together the cream cheese and 25 grams (2 tablespoons) of the lemon juice until well combined.

3 Add the dill, salt, pepper, and lemon zest.

4 Gently mix the salmon, capers, and scallions into the spread until well combined.

5 Transfer to a piping bag, pipe onto macaron shells, and serve immediately.

TIP: Mixing the cream cheese and lemon juice well creates a smooth spread and prevents the lemon juice from altering the texture of the smoked salmon. Mix thoroughly.

NOTES

Make the shells for this filling with no modifications or flavors. Reduce the confectioners' sugar content by 20 percent. Color them however you like. Leave them open-faced to control sweetness or sandwich with another shell.

The filling will stay fresh in the fridge for 1 week or will keep in the freezer for 1 month.

VARIATIONS

Pipe your shells into rings, like bagels, to resemble the real deal. For a super-fancy presentation, top the filling with a little dollop of crème fraîche, caviar, and gold leaf.

Recipes for Extra Yolks

There was a time when I rarely tried to use every bit of my ingredients. But thinking about the impact of compounded food waste and how my actions weren't aligning with my values quickly changed that carelessness. Making macarons leaves a lot of extra egg yolks, so put them to good use with these recipes.

If you're not sure how you want to use them, the yolks freeze nicely. Add two yolks to a sealable plastic snack bag, seal it, and freeze for later use.

German Buttercream

This recipe uses only one egg yolk, but it creates a silky, smooth, custardy filling for your macarons.

PREP TIME: 10 minutes

COOK TIME: 20 minutes, plus cooling time

TOTAL TIME: 3 hours 30 minutes

MAKES: filling for 36 macarons (1½-inch diameter) or frosting for 12 cupcakes

OCCASIONS: Oktoberfest, Halloween, Thanksgiving, Christmas

---

300 grams (1¼ cups) whole milk

½ teaspoon vanilla extract, plus more to taste

1 egg yolk

25 grams (2 tablespoons) granulated white sugar

15 grams (2 tablespoons) cornstarch

225 grams (1 cup) salted butter, room temperature

Confectioners' sugar (optional)

TIP: In step 3, pouring slowly will prevent making scrambled eggs.

NOTE

In an airtight container, the buttercream will stay fresh in the fridge for 2 weeks or will keep in the freezer for 3 months. If freezing, bring buttercream to room temperature for 1 hour and rewhip before piping.

1   First, make the pastry cream. In a medium saucepan over high heat, stir 240 grams (1 cup) of the milk and the vanilla extract until the mixture just starts to simmer, about 3 minutes. Remove from heat.

2   In a medium bowl, whisk together the remaining 60 grams (¼ cup) of milk, egg yolk, sugar, and cornstarch.

3   While whisking vigorously, slowly pour the hot milk into the egg mixture.

4   Return the mixture to the saucepan, increase the heat to high, and whisk constantly until the mixture thickens and comes to a boil, about 5 minutes.

5   Pour the mixture through a strainer and back into the bowl. Place plastic wrap directly on the custard to prevent a skin from forming.

6   Let the custard cool to room temperature, then refrigerate for 2 hours to set.

7   Remove from the fridge and let come to room temperature for 1 hour.

8   Using a stand mixer fitted with the paddle attachment or a hand mixer in a medium mixing bowl, beat the butter on high until pale and fluffy, about 3 minutes.

9   Add the custard to the butter 15 grams (1 tablespoon) at a time and continue beating to incorporate well.

10   Taste and add more vanilla and/or confectioners' sugar if desired.

11   Continue beating until smooth and fluffy, 2 to 3 more minutes.

VARIATIONS

Flavor this base with jams, liquid flavorings, pulverized cereal, or freeze-dried fruit. See Macaron Shell Flavors (page 32) for ideas.

Salted Egg Yolks

Food always brings my family together. Every fall, to celebrate the Mid-Autumn Festival, we enjoy moon cakes. The pastries have a soft caramelized shell and a thick paste inside, sometimes with additional fillings, such as salted egg yolks, red bean paste, nuts, or white lotus paste. My favorite moon cakes contain salted egg yolks, which have grown in popularity in America. They flavor potato chips and, when shaved like truffles, can be used to top pasta.

PREP TIME: 5 minutes

TOTAL TIME: 2 weeks

YIELD VARIES

OCCASIONS: dinner parties, Chinese New Year, Mid-Autumn Festival

75 grams (¼ cup) kosher salt per yolk

Egg yolks

TIP: Table salt contains anti-caking additives that can interrupt the curing process, so use kosher salt.

1 In a glass baking dish or plastic container, pour ½ inch of salt.

2 Use the back of a spoon or a whole egg in its shell to create divots, at least ¼ inch apart, for each yolk.

3 Gently place the yolks in the divots.

4 Gently pour more salt over the eggs to cover them completely.

5 Refrigerate to cure for 1 week.

6 Remove the yolks, dust off the excess salt, and wrap the yolks in cheesecloth.

7 In the refrigerator or a dark place cooler than 50°F (10°C), hang the cheesecloth with the yolks to dry for 7 to 10 days.

> **NOTES**
>
> Use intact yolks with as much of the whites removed as possible. When you cover the yolks with salt, you shouldn't be able to see the yolks at all anymore.
>
> In an airtight container, store the cured yolks in the fridge until ready to use, up to 2 weeks, or store them in the freezer for up to 6 months.

VARIATION

If you don't have a kitchen torch, use your oven's broiler. Turn it on high and let broil for about 2 minutes, keeping an eye on it the whole time. Sugar can scorch within seconds.

Yuzu Raspberry Crème Brûlée

A citrus fruit, yuzu originated in China but grew to international popularity through Japanese cuisine. For the longest time, the idea of crème brûlée intimidated me. Restaurants make it, so it must be hard to make, right? *Wrong!* These crowd-pleasers come together easily, and the bright acidity of the fruit balances the creamy custard.

PREP TIME: 10 minutes

COOK TIME: 45 minutes

TOTAL TIME: 5 hours

SERVES: 12

OCCASIONS: dinner parties, anniversaries, Valentine's Day, Mother's Day, Christmas, New Year's Eve, baby showers

---

500 grams (2 cups) heavy cream

65 grams (⅓ cup) granulated white sugar, plus 65 grams (⅓ cup) for topping

1 teaspoon vanilla bean paste

4 egg yolks

60 grams (¼ cup) yuzu juice

30 grams (¼ cup) cornstarch

75 grams (½ cup) fresh raspberries

NOTES

Covered, the crèmes brûlées will stay fresh in the fridge for 5 days. In an airtight container, they will stay fresh in the freezer for 2 months. If freezing, thaw in the fridge overnight before topping with sugar and torching or broiling.

1 Preheat the oven to 320°F (160°C).

2 In a medium saucepan over medium heat, combine the heavy cream and sugar, stirring occasionally, until it simmers, about 5 minutes. Sift in the cornstarch and stir to combine until no chunks remain. Remove from heat.

3 In a medium bowl, whisk together the vanilla bean paste, egg yolks, and yuzu juice until well combined.

4 While whisking, slowly pour in the hot cream in a steady stream. Continue whisking until the mixture combines well.

5 Strain the mixture through a sieve to remove any lumps.

6 Divide the raspberries evenly among 12 ramekins.

7 Pour the custard mixture over the raspberries, filling each ramekin almost to the top.

8 Add hot water to 1 large or 2 smaller baking dishes and place the ramekins in the water, which should reach halfway up the sides of the ramekins.

9 Bake until the custard sets but still jiggles slightly in the middle, 30 to 35 minutes.

10 Remove the ramekins from the water bath and let cool to room temperature.

11 Refrigerate until completely chilled, at least 4 hours.

12 When ready to serve, sprinkle 1 teaspoon of the topping sugar over each ramekin.

13 Using a kitchen torch, melt and caramelize the sugar until it turns golden brown and bubbles. Serve immediately.

3

Decorated Sugar Cookies

My sugar cookie adventures had a rocky start: made with saccharine, shaped into a ribbon, slathered in pink egg wash. One shape, one color, dubious results. But that experience didn't make me throw in the kitchen towel. It inspired me to try again and do better. My sugar cookies have come a long way. Use them as inspiration for your own successes.

A SHORT INTRODUCTION TO DECORATED SUGAR COOKIES

Keep these notes in mind when making, handling, storing, and freezing your sugar cookies.

- Don't overwork the dough. Gluten can cause all kinds of surprises, including misshapen cutouts. The moment the dough comes together and looks uniform, stop! You're done. Remember: minimum effort for maximum impact.

- You can batch dough ahead of time for future use. Wrap it, airtight, in plastic and store in the fridge for up to 1 week or in the freezer for up to 3 months. When baking from frozen, defrost the dough in the fridge overnight.

- Store baked, uniced cookies in an airtight container on the counter for up to 2 days or keep them in the freezer for up to 2 months.

- Decorate baked cookies after they have cooled completely or, if frozen, have come to room temperature. If decorating while fresh, ice them within 2 days of baking to prevent them from drying out. But take into consideration whether you under-baked or overbaked your cookies and the humidity of your environment. At room temperature, underbaked cookies have a longer working time without drying out. Overbaked cookies will dry out faster, so you'll need to decorate and package them within 24 hours.

- To ensure that your icing dries, keep decorated cookies uncovered. Royal Icing (page 70) needs airflow to dry. If you cover your cookies, they're not going to dry.

- You can freeze baked, iced, and dried cookies, too. Heat-seal them individually in cellophane or polyethylene wrappers and freeze them in airtight containers for up to 4 months. To defrost without ruining the icing, let them come to room temperature for 3 hours in the airtight container to prevent condensation from forming.

- When in doubt, test it out. If you're not sure whether something will work or how something will behave, try it. Take notes. Assess the results and, as necessary, try again.

Vanilla Spice Sugar Cookies

In 2018, these fluffy cookies earned the grand prize on Food Network's *Christmas Cookie Challenge*. Straight from the oven, their texture feels light, fluffy, and tender, with a slight crisp around the edge. Decorated and stored, the texture homogenizes to a more consistent chewiness throughout the cookie.

PREP TIME: 15 minutes
COOK TIME: 10 minutes, plus resting and cooling time
TOTAL TIME: 3 hours
MAKES: 24 cookies (3-inch diameter)
OCCASIONS: Oktoberfest, Halloween, Thanksgiving, Christmas

450 grams (3 cups) all-purpose flour

¼ teaspoon ground nutmeg

⅓ teaspoon ground cardamom

½ teaspoon ground cinnamon

170 grams (6 ounces) salted butter, room temperature

200 grams (1 cup) granulated white sugar

¾ teaspoon baking powder

1 teaspoon vanilla extract

2 large eggs, room temperature

1. In a medium bowl, sift together the flour and spices and set aside.

2. In the bowl of a stand mixer fitted with the paddle attachment, cream the butter, sugar, baking powder, and vanilla extract on medium speed until well combined and slightly fluffy, about 2 minutes.

3. One at a time, add the eggs, beating to incorporate each addition fully.

4. Continue beating until the mixture becomes lighter and fluffier, 2 more minutes.

5. All at once, add the dry ingredients and mix on low until dough forms and naturally pulls away from the bowl. Scrape down the sides of the bowl at least once to incorporate everything fully.

6. Halve the dough.

7. Roll out each half to 1 inch thick and wrap in plastic wrap.

8. Let the dough rest in the refrigerator for 2 hours before rolling.

(recipe continues)

NOTE

Chilling the dough before baking helps relax the gluten, which results in a better cutout shape. It's also much easier to work with chilled dough. You don't need extra flour to roll out the dough or to use on the cookie cutter(s).

VARIATION

For fewer but slightly thicker cookies, roll the dough out to ⅜ inch. Vary the spices in your cookies for different flavors; for example, try it with five-spice powder!

9   When ready to bake, preheat the oven to 375°F (190°C).

10 Open each plastic wrap covering the dough, add another sheet of plastic wrap atop the dough, and roll both sets of dough out to ¼ inch thick.

11 Using cookie cutters, cut out the raw cookies and place them on silicone baking mats on baking or cookie sheets.

12 Reroll the scraps and cut out shapes until you use all the dough (see Tips).

13 Bake until the centers dome slightly and the edges turn barely golden, about 9 minutes for smaller cookies, 11 minutes for larger cookies.

14 On the baking mats on the baking sheets, let the cookies cool to room temperature before icing.

TIPS: In step 12, when rerolling the dough to use all the scraps, try not to reroll it too much. Overworked gluten can result in misshapen cookies.

Adjust baking time based on cookie thickness and texture preference. Thinner or softer cookies need less time. Thicker or crispier cookies need more time.

Cooling them on a cooling rack will dry them out a bit, as well. These cookies have a large, open crumb structure—which means they dry out quickly and have a shorter shelf life—so enjoy them sooner than later!

Lemon Vanilla Sugar Cookies

This cutout recipe evolved from two years of experimentation with ingredients, ratios, and flavors to achieve my preferred balance of spread, texture, and taste. Depending on thickness and baking time, the cookies can end up soft and chewy or a bit firmer with caramelization.

PREP TIME: 15 minutes
COOK TIME: 12 minutes, plus resting and cooling time
TOTAL TIME: 3 hours
MAKES: 36 cookies (3-inch diameter)
OCCASIONS: birthdays, Easter, Independence Day, bridal showers, baby showers

600 grams (4 cups) all-purpose flour

20 grams (3 tablespoons) cornstarch

225 grams (8 ounces) salted butter, room temperature

300 grams (1½ cups) granulated white sugar

½ teaspoon baking powder

50 grams (2¼ tablespoons) honey of choice

2 teaspoons vanilla bean paste

2 teaspoons lemon zest

15 grams (1 tablespoon) vegetable glycerin (optional; keeps cookies moister for longer)

2 large eggs, room temperature

1 In a medium bowl, sift together the flour and cornstarch and set aside.

2 In the bowl of a stand mixer, cream the butter, sugar, baking powder, honey, vanilla bean paste, lemon zest, and glycerin, if using, on medium speed until well combined and slightly fluffy, about 2 minutes.

3 One at a time, add the eggs, beating to incorporate each addition fully.

4 Continue beating until the mixture becomes lighter and fluffier, 2 more minutes.

5 All at once, add the dry ingredients and mix on low until dough forms and naturally pulls away from the bowl. Scrape down the sides of the bowl at least once to incorporate everything fully.

6 Halve the dough.

7 Roll out each half to 1 inch thick and wrap in plastic wrap (see Tips).

8 Let the dough rest in the refrigerator for 2 hours before rolling.

(recipe continues)

NOTES

Chilling the dough before baking helps relax the gluten, which results in a better cutout shape. It's also much easier to work with chilled dough. You don't need extra flour to roll out the dough or use on the cookie cutter(s).

You can make the dough in advance and freeze it for up to 6 months.

Store it in an airtight container and defrost in the fridge overnight before baking. In an airtight container, baked cookies stay fresh for 1 week on the counter, or you can store them in the freezer for 3 months.

9   When ready to bake, preheat the oven to 375°F (190°C).

10 Open the plastic wrap covering each dough, add another sheet of plastic wrap atop the dough, and roll both sets of dough out to ¼ inch thick.

11 Using cookie cutters, cut out the raw cookies and place them on silicone baking mats on baking or cookie sheets.

12 Reroll the scraps and cut out shapes until you use all the dough.

13 Bake until the centers dome slightly and the edges turn barely golden, 10 to 11 minutes for smaller cookies, 11 to 12 minutes for larger cookies.

14 On the baking mats on the baking sheets, let the cookies cool to room temperature before icing.

TIPS: If heat-sealing individual cookies in cellophane or polyethylene wrappers, the vegetable glycerin in the recipe helps extend room-temperature shelf life to weeks.

In step 12, when rerolling the dough to use all the scraps, try not to reroll it too much. Overworked gluten can result in misshapen cookies.

Adjust baking time based on cookie thickness and texture preference. Thinner or softer cookies need less time. Thicker or crispier cookies need more time. Cooling them on a cooling rack will dry them out a bit, as well.

(recipe continues)

VARIATIONS

For fewer but slightly thicker cookies, roll out the dough to ⅜ inch. Underbaking gives these cookies a softer, chewier texture. The edges should brown only very slightly, and the bottom should just start to become golden.

Lemon zest gives these cookies a nice brightness, but you can omit it with no other changes to the recipe to create Vanilla Sugar Cookies. For Matcha Sugar Cookies, replace 25 grams of the flour with 25 grams of sifted matcha (about 1 tablespoon of each), use the same amount of vanilla extract instead of vanilla bean paste, and omit the lemon zest. For Ube Sugar Cookies, replace the vanilla bean paste with 2 teaspoons of ube extract and omit the lemon zest. For Black Sesame Sugar Cookies, replace 25 grams (1 tablespoon) of the flour with 50 grams (3 tablespoons) of pulverized toasted black sesame seeds, use the same amount of vanilla extract instead of vanilla bean paste, and omit the lemon zest.

Instead of Royal Icing (page 70), try topping these cookies with Vanilla Sesame Glaze (page 11), Lychee Buttercream (page 38), or White Chocolate Ganache Filling (page 42).

Red Velvet Sugar Cookies

In the 1800s, bakers refined their cakes from a coarser crumb structure to a softer, "velvet" texture, which created velvet cake. From regular chocolate cake, devil's food cake evolved around 1900, with more chocolate added, making it darker and heavier. Using non-Dutched cocoa instead of chocolate resulted in a reddish color, giving us red velvet cake. Translating that dish into other desserts doesn't always work, but it does in this case. These cookies chew much softer than other roll-out cookies and have a tender, cake-like, open crumb structure. Handle with care.

PREP TIME: 15 minutes
COOK TIME: 13 minutes, plus resting and cooling time
TOTAL TIME: 3 hours
MAKES: 24 cookies (3-inch diameter)
OCCASIONS: Valentine's Day, Chinese New Year, Christmas

420 grams (2¾ cups) all-purpose flour

30 grams (2 tablespoons) cocoa powder

2 teaspoons cornstarch

225 grams (1 cup) salted butter, room temperature

120 grams (½ cup) cream cheese

100 grams (½ cup) granulated white sugar

90 grams (⅔ cup) confectioners' sugar

1 teaspoon baking powder

1½ teaspoons cream of tartar

½ teaspoon vanilla extract

1 egg, room temperature

7 to 10 drops red gel food coloring or ⅛ teaspoon red powdered food coloring

1 In a medium bowl, sift together the flour, cocoa, and cornstarch and set aside.

2 In the bowl of a stand mixer fitted with the paddle attachment, cream the butter, cream cheese, sugars, baking powder, cream of tartar, and vanilla extract on low speed, gradually increasing to medium, until well incorporated, about 3 minutes. The mixture will start to fluff as it incorporates air.

3 Add the egg and beat on low until the mixture becomes viscous, 30 to 45 seconds.

4 Increase the mixer speed to medium and beat until the mixture becomes lighter and fluffier, about 2 more minutes.

5 All at once, add the dry ingredients and food coloring and mix on low until dough forms and naturally pulls away from the bowl. Scrape down the sides of the bowl at least once to incorporate everything fully. The dough should feel smooth and soft, almost like Play-Doh.

(recipe continues)

NOTES

Before adding the dry ingredients, you want a wet, well-incorporated batter with just a bit of air in it. Chilling the dough before baking helps relax the gluten, which results in a better cutout shape. It's also much easier to work with chilled dough.

VARIATIONS

For fewer but slightly thicker cookies, roll out the dough to ⅜ inch.

For Red Velvet Passion Fruit Sugar Cookies, replace the cream of tartar with 2 teaspoons of passion fruit powder.

Instead of Royal Icing (page 70), try topping these cookies with Cream Cheese Filling (page 39) or Chocolate Ganache Filling (page 41).

6   Halve the dough.

7   Roll out each half to ½ inch thick and wrap in plastic wrap.

8   Let the dough rest in the refrigerator for at least 2 hours before rolling.

9   When ready to bake, preheat the oven to 375°F (190°C).

10 Remove the dough from the refrigerator to warm for 10 minutes.

11 Roll both sets of dough to ¼ inch thick.

12 Using cookie cutters, cut out the raw cookies and place them on silicone baking mats on baking or cookie sheets.

13 Reroll the scraps and cut out shapes until you use all the dough (see Tips).

14 Keeping the cookies on the baking mats on the baking sheets, place them in the freezer for 5 minutes before baking.

15 Bake until the centers just start to dome, 10 to 11 minutes for smaller cookies, 12 to 13 minutes for larger cookies.

16 On the baking mats on the sheets, let the cookies cool to room temperature before icing.

TIPS: Use high-quality cocoa powder, such as the Valrhona brand.

Use more or less food coloring based on your judgment or preference.

In step 13, when rerolling the dough to use all the scraps, try not to reroll it too much. Overworked gluten can result in misshapen cookies.

Adjust baking time based on cookie thickness and texture preference. Thinner or softer cookies need less time. Thicker or crispier cookies need more time. Cooling them on a cooling rack will dry them out a bit, as well.

Royal Icing

In the early 1700s, royal icing replaced an earlier style even more like a traditional meringue. The first written reference to it appears in a British confectionery cookbook published in 1770, and bakers started piping it in the 1840s. Traditional recipes use egg whites as a base, which can dry to a hard, tooth-cracking density. This recipe aligns with modern versions that contain meringue powder and corn syrup, which result in a softer bite. As a base, it's supposed to be thick, with modifications to achieve smoother consistencies.

PREP TIME: 5 minutes
COOK TIME: 3 minutes
TOTAL TIME: 8 minutes
MAKES: icing for 50 cookies
(3-inch diameter)

900 grams (7½ cups)
  confectioners' sugar

120 grams (½ cup) warm water,
  plus more as needed

60 grams (4 tablespoons)
  meringue powder

1 teaspoon vanilla extract

½ teaspoon cream of tartar or
  white gel food coloring

50 grams (2½ tablespoons)
  light corn syrup

1   Sift the confectioners' sugar and attach the paddle attachment to a stand mixer.

2   In the bowl of the stand mixer, whisk together by hand the ½ cup of warm water and the meringue powder until the mixture froths with big bubbles and most of the meringue powder has dissolved, with nothing stuck to the sides of the bowl.

3   All at once, add the remaining ingredients and mix on low speed. The mixture will feel *very* stiff and may not come together yet.

4   Using 1 tablespoon at a time, add more warm water and continue mixing on low until the icing develops the consistency of thick toothpaste. It still should feel very stiff. This is your base icing.

5   When ready to decorate, remove the amount needed and add gel food coloring and enough water to achieve the desired consistency.

TIPS: If, at any stage, you add too much water, add a bit more confectioners' sugar to balance it.

If you're creating three-dimensional elements, such as flowers, at the end of step 4 beat your base icing on high until it becomes fluffy like buttercream, about 2 minutes. Doing so makes the icing *much* easier to pipe and results in airier icing when dried. It should crumble slightly like a meringue cookie.

Pipe only with room-temperature icing so you know that it has the right consistency. Use only the amount needed for a given project and store the rest.

NOTES

The cream of tartar or white food coloring offsets the brown tinge from the vanilla extract. It also discourages color bleed.

Your base icing shouldn't appear translucent, a dead giveaway for underbeaten icing in which the meringue powder hasn't activated fully. If translucent, the icing will bleed more easily and prove harder to work with, so beat it some more. If your base icing looks porous and isn't drying, you likely overbeat it. The meringue powder has so much air in it that it's turning into meringue. You need to start over.

Humidity *hugely* affects icing. In California, where the air runs dry in the summer, icing dries completely and cookies can stack after about 8 hours. On the East Coast and around the Gulf of Mexico, high humidity levels can push drying time up to 48 hours. Your drying time will vary.

In an airtight container, store extra icing in the refrigerator for up to 2 weeks or in the freezer for up to 4 months. If you freeze it for later use, let it come to room temperature and stir before use.

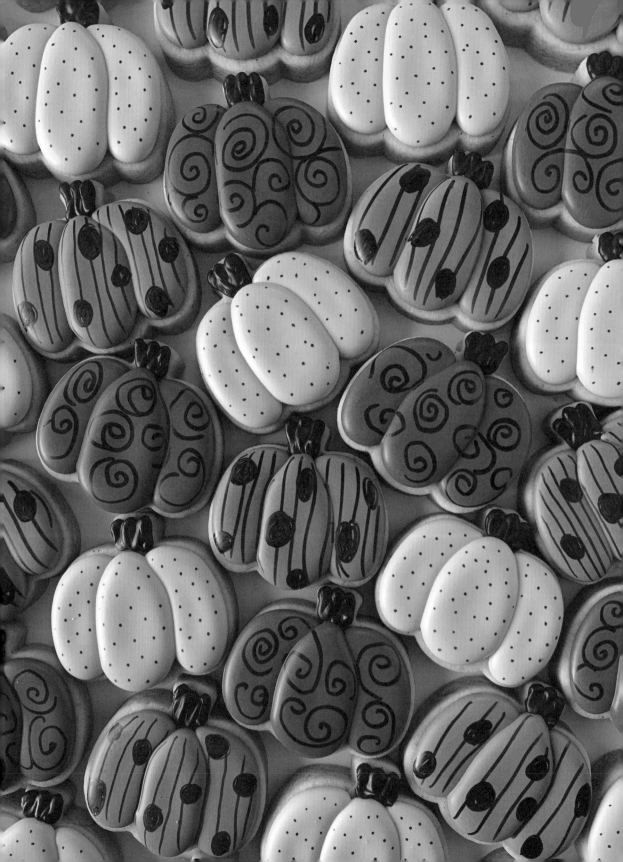

Decorating Sugar Cookies

In the last several years, cookie decorating has reached new heights. But the basics, always the most important skills, remain the same. After you master those, the possibilities become endless. The most popular, most aesthetically pleasing cookies aren't necessarily the most complex or detailed. Cleanly decorated cookies often look simple, but it takes a *lot* of skill to get them exactly right. As you'll see, my style focuses on clean work and consistent execution.

Tools, Colorings, and Consistencies

To start your cookie-decorating journey, you need some basic tools and supplies. Everyone has their favorites, including me. Here's what I suggest.

Decorating Tools

- **Bowls,** whether mixing bowls or regular ones, hold your icing for mixing and decorating.

- **Cookie cutters,** whether metal or plastic, come in an overwhelming array of options. If you can imagine it, someone has made it into a cookie cutter. To get started, buy a bundle from your local craft store or Amazon.

- **Dehydrators or fans** increase airflow, which, if you put one on the lowest setting, makes Royal Icing (page 70) dry faster and shinier. While not necessary, using one will help you work faster and more efficiently.

- **Lazy Susans, turntables, or cookie swivels** aren't a must for beginners. They help you rotate cookies easily so you don't need to move your hands or body, which proves especially handy when creating floral cookies.

- **Piping bags,** whether disposable or reusable, all behave a bit differently. Expect a learning curve for handling either kind. The Borderlands Bakery online shop offers robust, comfortable piping bags.

- **Piping tips** pipe stiff icing so that it holds a specific shape, such as stars, leaves, and other designs.

- **Scissors** are for trimming piping bags. Sharp embroidery scissors cut cleanly across piping bag tips.

- **Scribe tools, metal cocktail skewers, or needles** help maneuver icing, pop air bubbles, and fix mistakes. If investing in a scribe tool, look for one with a scraper, which makes fixing those inevitable mistakes much easier. Icing sticks to wood, so no wooden skewers or toothpicks.

If you're going to package your finished cookies, invest in food-safe cellophane or polyethylene bags and a heat sealer to keep the cookies fresher longer.

Food Colorings

Food colorings behave like hair dye. Tone deepens over time. If you want bright red, stop a few shades before the desired tone, wait 30 minutes for it to develop, and adjust. After you understand how your colors behave, you can eliminate the wait. Oversaturation risks color bleed and brittle icing.

- **Gels** color icing easily for beginners. Use a little bit at a time, building tone slowly as you learn how each color behaves because, even if from the same manufacturer, they all behave differently.

- **Powders** are gaining popularity because they contain more pigment but less flavor than gels. Powders usually require activation with a few drops of water to reach full potential and blend without streaking. But baker beware. The moment a wet sponge or towel touches *any* small speck of it, the color will activate, potentially staining something you can't clean easily. Powders work wonders in macarons. Very little product will color shells vibrantly.

- **Edible glitter** is self-explanatory, but never mix it into icing. Always place it on top for maximum impact and minimal waste. (Glitter doesn't count if you can't see it.) Apply after the icing has crusted but before it has dried through so that the glitter adheres.

- **Luster dusts** are another kind of topical pigment. Dry-buff them onto your icing or mix them with alcohol or another food-grade activator to create a metallic look on icing or cookies.

- **Food markers,** while not a necessity, allow you to draw guides on naked cookies or apply fine details to dry icing. If adding them to your coloring kit, invest in a set of various colors. Look for the dual-tipped variety to get two different ink thicknesses.

Icing Consistencies

The consistency of your icing will make or break your cookies. This part of the cookie decorating process takes longest to learn. Not only do ingredients affect consistency but also, of course, environment and technique. Give yourself plenty of time to get the hang of it. The learning curve may feel steep and frustrating, which is totally normal. Keep trying and don't give up.

Everyone has a preferred style for decorating. Different cookie artists use different methods to achieve similar results. When it comes to flooding, which means completely covering a surface, some decorators prefer a stiffer outline icing consistency (like toothpaste) and a looser flood consistency (like honey). But for efficiency's sake, I like to use a single consistency for both the outline and the flood. There's no

right or wrong way to do it. Try a variety of approaches and go with what works best for you. See examples on on page 71.

Outlining and Flooding Consistency

For covering surfaces, the consistency of the icing should flow like honey but not thinner. To achieve this consistency, slowly add water to loosen the base icing. For better control, use a spray bottle or pipette. The thinner the consistency, the greater the risk of icing running off the cookies, not holding shape, and the colors bleeding. Air bubbles can result if you mix too much. A good flood settles with a slight jiggle or with the assistance of your scribe tool.

Detail Consistency

This icing consistency—used for lines, text, or piped details—resembles loose toothpaste and doesn't settle on its own.

Stiff Consistency

For piping borders that keep their shape and for stenciling, this icing consistency looks like standard toothpaste.

Floral Consistency

While floral consistency looks almost indistinguishable from stiff consistency, it feels more like buttercream, making it much easier to pipe in large quantities than stiff consistency. To achieve floral consistency, double the corn syrup in the recipe for Royal Icing (page 70) and beat the base icing on high until it fluffs, about 2 extra minutes. Overbeating icing makes it porous, which usually you don't want, but it pipes more easily and provides a softer bite. It's fluffier, so don't stack the finished cookies.

Decorating Techniques

Mastering a few basic techniques will allow you to create almost any design imaginable. But my techniques aren't the only way. So many incredible artists share their work on social media. Check them out and learn from them. The world is your cookie, so decorate it!

Loading and Trimming the Piping Bag

For Royal Icing (page 70), I use disposable piping bags, but you can use reusable bags, a squeeze bottle with a piping tip, or even a plastic storage bag in a pinch. Try everything that seems viable to determine what you like. Disposable piping bags come in a triangular shape with a closed tip. Use a cup or jar to hold the bag when filling, then secure it with a bag clip or tie a knot to close it.

To pipe without a piping tip, fill the bag with icing and secure it. Flatten the tip, aligning the seam down the center of the bag. Trim straight across, 1 millimeter or less to start. Start small and increase after some practice. The bigger the hole, the more icing will flow out. The smaller the hole, the less icing will flow out. If the hole runs too small, your icing may curl. If your hole is too big, you may end up with air bubbles in your flood icing or the icing will become difficult to control. Find the right balance for you by practicing.

Outlining and Lines

To pipe a line or a border, hold the piping bag at a 45-degree angle, seam facing up, or lined up with your fingertips. Apply gentle, even pressure so the icing emerges from the piping bag, and let it adhere to the surface of the cookie. At the same time, drag the piping bag, keeping distance between it and the cookie surface, and let the icing fall smoothly in a path behind your hand. Piping too closely to the cookie makes it harder to create a smooth, clean line. Practice on paper first until the technique feels comfortable.

Flooding

Using the same consistency as your outline, keep your piping bag perpendicular to the cookie and squeeze hard. As you apply pressure to the bag, icing will pool around the tip. As you flood the cookie, don't make spaghetti strings, which will create air bubbles.

Using a Scribe

Despite best efforts to the contrary, flooding a cookie sometimes results in air bubbles, uneven icing, or icing that runs over the edge. Having a scribe for these situations will help. Use the sharp end of the scribe to clean edges or pop air bubbles. When popping air bubbles, oscillate your scribe either in tiny circles or a back-and-forth motion. Don't pull the scribe up from the icing. Drag it to the side so as not to leave peaks or create new air bubbles.

Leaf Details

Load the piping bag with icing that has a toothpaste-like consistency. With the seam down the middle of the bag, trim your tip so it forms a point but lies flat, and then trim each side of the tip diagonally and symmetrically so it looks like a nib on a giant fountain pen. By applying different amounts of pressure and by moving your hand either back or forth or in one direction, you can achieve a variety of leaves: small leaves, chubby leaves, larges leaves, and even seaweed.

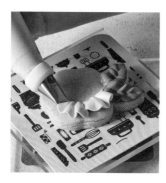 

Floral Details

Load floral-consistency icing into your piping bag, fitted with a piping tip of your choice. Use a tip such as 1M to create rosettes, and tips 101 and 104 to create petals. When creating petals, it's helpful to use a cookie turntable as you pipe. Experiment with a variety of piping tips and piping techniques to create different floral looks.

Beaded Borders

With toothpaste-like consistency icing in the piping bag, trim the tip as usual but make a larger hole. The size of the hole depends on the size of the beads that you want to make.

Piping Tip Details

You can use piping tips with tipless piping bags. Just drop your tip into the base of the bag, taking care that the tip doesn't cut the bag on the way down, and trim the bag so that the tip pokes through.

Wet on Wet

This technique uses multiple colors of icing with the same flood consistency to create designs that settle flat. Pipe the base layer, then add on additional layers of icing immediately without waiting for the first layer to dry so they all settle into a single layer as the icing dries.

Layering

You can build multiple layers of icing on a cookie in endless ways, incorporating lots of other techniques and even other edible materials. Wait until each layer crusts over to add more layers to create dimension and separation.

Painting

When icing has dried, you can paint it! Create watercolor designs, multidimensional marvels, and even full-on artwork cookies by mixing gel or powder coloring (page 75) with a high-proof, clear alcohol such as vodka or grain alcohol. You can also use a color activator like Sugar Art's Color Solution, which turns powder pigments (such as petal dusts and luster dusts) into paints. This particular formula works like makeup primer, giving you more working time than if using alcohol, making it a great option for techniques that require more time to complete or for seamlessly blending colors. Ratios differ depending on each constituent in the edible paint, so have fun playing around with painting your cookies.

Splattering

Load a small brush with edible paint and flick it to create stylish splatters on the cookie.

Brush Embroidery

Working in sections so the icing doesn't dry too quickly, pipe details onto the cookie in semicircles or other curved shapes. Using a flat or angle brush turned to the side, drag the outline inward with small strokes to create a lacy look.

Stenciling

Using a traditional stencil or silkscreen stencil, you can scrape icing through it or airbrush through it to create gorgeous designs. Use a stencil holder to help keep your cookie and stencil in place.

Parchment Texture

With parchment paper, you can create wonderful modern textures. Crumble the paper, lay it on wet icing until it dries, and then peel it off. You also can buy embossed parchment papers for incredibly intricate or subtle designs.

Molded Details

Modeling chocolate or fondant in food-grade silicone molds creates consistent details that add texture, dimension, and interest to cookies. For ease of releasing, dust the molds with cornstarch before adding fondant. You can color your medium directly or paint over it. Double-check that the color will work with the medium. For example, candy color, which is fat soluble, won't mix with fondant properly, and gel color can cause chocolate to seize.

Drying and Storing

After decorating your cookies, let them dry *completely* before storing them totally uncovered. Royal icing needs airflow to dry. On a flat surface, place the cookies in a single layer and let them dry overnight or, depending on the humidity of your environment, longer. The part of California where I live has an average of 35 percent humidity, so I can bake, decorate, and package my cookies within 24 hours. In Florida, where the humidity runs much higher, the same cookies will take twice as long to dry. You can find out what's right for you only by doing the work. In an airtight container, you can store the completely dry cookies at room temperature for up to 1 week before they start drying out or going stale. To keep them fresher longer, heat-seal them in airtight cellophane bags.

Design Ideas

This section contains inspiration for all kinds of occasions, from dinner parties and birthdays to Chinese New Year and Christmas. Use this list and the accompanying photos to brainstorm and inspire your own cookie occasions and designs.

Frequent Occasions	Annual Occasions	Less Frequent Occasions
breakfast	birthdays	housewarmings
snacks	anniversaries	bridal showers
Shabbat	Super Bowl Sunday	bachelor/ette parties
dinner parties	Valentine's Day	weddings
book club	St. Patrick's Day	baby showers
girls' night	Chinese (or Lunar) New Year	
potlucks	Cherry Blossom Festival	
bake sales	Easter	
high tea	Derby Day	
cookouts	Cinco de Mayo	
picnics	Mother's Day	
hiking	Father's Day	
road trips	Pride	
	Independence Day	
	Mid-Autumn Festival	
	Rosh Hashanah	
	Oktoberfest	
	Halloween	
	Thanksgiving	
	Hanukkah	
	Christmas	
	New Year's Eve	

BOOK CLUB

BAKE SALES

HIGH TEA

PICNICS

CINCO DE MAYO

MOTHER'S DAY

MOTHER'S DAY

PRIDE

HALLOWEEN

THANKSGIVING

CHRISTMAS

NEW YEAR'S EVE

NEW YEAR'S EVE

HOUSEWARMINGS

BRIDAL SHOWERS

WEDDINGS

BABY SHOWERS

Troubleshooting Decorated Sugar Cookies

Sugar cookies sound deceptively easy, but—now that you know how to make and ice them—you know better! As with macarons, the full process involves so many parameters that only you can figure out what went wrong and how to fix it. Again, keep track of everything you do, change one parameter at a time, document your results, review, adjust, and test your hypothesis. A stable base icing will eliminate most of these issues, so as a first priority, make sure that your base icing is not over or under beaten. Once you're comfortable with the integrity of your base icing, following the tips in this section will shed some light onto what else might be going on if you're experiencing any of these symptoms. Use this overview to help you troubleshoot.

Air Bubbles

The base icing runs thick and doesn't beat for very long, so it shouldn't have many air bubbles. A few, sure, but if you're spending all your time popping bubbles, try this modification. Vigorously mixing loose icing can create air bubbles. If that's the case, you should be able to spot it immediately when mixing. Bang your bowl firmly on the counter a few times to bring bubbles to the surface and pop them. Another possibility is that your piping hole could be too big. Lots of air bubbles break as they exit the piping bag, but not if the hole is running big. It can feel tempting to cut a big hole for flooding, but anything wider than 1 millimeter likely will preserve bubbles.

Butter Bleed

If your icing develops oily patches, it likely comes from butter bleed, the process in which oils from the cookie leach into the icing. This problem can happen with under-baked cookies or if baked cookies become too warm and reactivate the residual fat.

Color Bleed

If icing colors bleed into one another, your icing is too loose or you've waited too long between piping colors. Moisture from the wet layer might have bled onto the dry side, bringing the color along with it. After you put down a layer and it crusts, quickly add the next layer.

Cratering

Little craters can appear in the icing after it has dried, which makes patching the holes particularly challenging in some cases, especially if they occur in small or narrow areas. To prevent this problem, you can employ a number of techniques. Use the thickest consistency of icing possible for that application, put a freshly decorated cookie under a fan or dehydrator to help it crust as fast as possible, or pipe a squiggle of thick icing underneath the spot(s) where cratering likely will occur.

Curled Icing

First, check that your piping bag seam isn't getting in the way and causing the curls. If it is, trim it or try another piping bag. When you pipe, that first bit of icing needs to adhere to something, or it will curl into itself. Touch it down quickly and evenly, then drag and drop it, allowing the icing to fall smoothly behind your hand.

Icing Won't Dry

You decorated your cookies, but the next day they're . . . *still* wet? First, check the humidity of your environment. The higher the water content of the ambient air, the longer the cookies will take to dry. You may have to exercise (more) patience. Also make sure that you let the cookies dry uncovered. Drying requires airflow. If you can rule out the possibilities of humidity and airflow, you may have added coloring or flavoring that contains fat, which will prevent icing from drying, or you overmixed the icing.

Lines Breaking

Loading your piping bag sometimes can introduce air bubbles, which is totally normal. These bubbles can cause line breaks when piping. It's really no problem. Pipe a teeny bit more icing where the line broke and use your scribe to smooth it out.

Streaky Icing

This problem usually results from inadequately mixed icing or from icing that has been sitting around for a while. After 45 minutes, icing starts to separate. In both cases, give your icing a good massage. You can do that in the piping bag, or you can dump it out and remix before using.

4

Drop Cookies

I don't remember my first chocolate chip cookie, but in high school my friends and I hung out at the mall, where the heavenly scents of Mrs. Fields cookies wafted through the air, so good and so comforting. These recipes range from classics with a twist to cookies inspired by my heritage, blending East and West.

Miso Pecan Chocolate Chip Cookies

When introducing new flavors to your repertoire, it makes good sense to combine them with something familiar. These treats start as browned butter chocolate chip cookies, but the added miso paste brings a subtle savory saltiness and the crunchy pecans give a rich nuttiness.

PREP TIME: 15 minutes

COOK TIME: 15 minutes, plus cooling time

TOTAL TIME: 50 minutes

MAKES: 12 large cookies

OCCASIONS: Shabbat, book club, picnics, hiking, road trips, birthdays, Easter, Father's Day, Mid-Autumn Festival, Rosh Hashanah, Halloween, Thanksgiving

225 grams (1 cup) unsalted butter

100 grams (½ cup) granulated white sugar

100 grams (½ packed cup) light brown sugar

2 large eggs, room temperature

1 teaspoon vanilla extract

15 grams (1 tablespoon) white miso paste

250 grams (1⅔ cups) all-purpose flour

1 teaspoon baking soda

1 teaspoon kosher salt

170 grams (1½ cups) roasted pecans

165 grams (1 cup) bittersweet chocolate chips

1 Preheat the oven to 350°F (177°C) and line a baking sheet or cookie sheet with parchment paper.

2 In a saucepan over medium heat, melt the butter, stirring constantly, until it turns brown and smells nutty, about 5 minutes. Remove from heat and let cool for about 7 minutes.

3 In a large mixing bowl, use a spatula to stir the white sugar, brown sugar, and cooled brown butter until well combined.

4 Stir in the eggs, vanilla extract, and miso paste until smooth.

5 In a medium bowl, sift together the flour, baking soda, and salt.

6 Gradually add the dry ingredients to the wet ingredients, stirring until just combined.

7 Rough-chop the pecans.

8 Fold the chopped pecans and chocolate chips into the dough.

9 Divide the dough into 12 equal portions, roll the portions between your hands into balls, and place the raw cookies on the prepared baking sheet, leaving about 2 inches on all sides of each cookie.

10 Bake until the centers set and the edges turn golden brown, 12 to 15 minutes.

11 On the baking sheet, let the cookies cool for 5 minutes before transferring them to a wire rack to cool completely to room temperature.

> **NOTES**
>
> The dough freezes well. In an airtight container, store the dough balls in the freezer for up to 3 months. Bake from frozen and add 3 more minutes to the bake time. In an airtight container, baked cookies will stay fresh in the freezer for 2 months.

VARIATIONS

For Browned Butter Miso Cookies, omit the pecans and chocolate chips. You can also experiment with mix-ins: toasted hazelnuts instead of pecans or almonds, and butterscotch chips instead of chocolate chips.

Ube Melting Moments

In recent years, ube, a purple yam from southeast Asia, has become insanely popular in America. Trader Joe's, for example, rolls out ube cookies, pancake mix, ice cream, and more. If you haven't tried it yet, it tastes pistachio adjacent, vanilla-y, and slightly coconutty. It sounds richly decadent, but ube contains lots of nutrients and almost no fat. It's hard to capture the flavor with just the yam, but a concentrated extract expresses its distinct flavor. These cookies have the same buttery taste and mouthfeel as shortbread, except they run lighter and more crumbly. They'll dissolve in your mouth as you enjoy them.

PREP TIME: 15 minutes
COOK TIME: 13 minutes, plus freezing and cooling time
TOTAL TIME: 1 hour 15 minutes
MAKES: 36 small cookies
OCCASIONS: dinner parties, girls' night, bake sales, Mother's Day, Halloween, bridal showers, baby showers

225 grams (1 cup) salted butter

150 grams (1 cup) confectioners' sugar, plus more for rolling

15 grams (1 tablespoon) vanilla pudding powder

2 teaspoons ube extract

100 grams (¾ cup) cornstarch

150 grams (1 cup) all-purpose flour

TIP: It may take some trial and error to determine when they finish cooking. If they're browning, they're overdone. They should remain the same color throughout baking.

1 Preheat the oven to 350°F (177°C) and line a baking tray with parchment paper or a silicone mat.

2 In a microwave-safe dish, partially melt the butter by microwaving it on high for 10 to 15 seconds.

3 In the bowl of a stand mixer fitted with a paddle attachment or using a hand mixer in a medium mixing bowl, cream the butter, sugar, pudding powder, and ube extract on medium until well combined and slightly fluffy, about 3 minutes.

4 Add the cornstarch and flour and continue mixing to form a smooth, soft dough, about 1 minute 30 seconds.

5 Using a 1-tablespoon ice cream scoop, melon baller, cookie scoop, or soup spoon, scoop the dough and roll the portions between your hands into balls. Place the balls on the silicone mat, 12 to a sheet, evenly spaced.

6 Freeze the dough balls until solid, about 20 minutes.

7 Bake until just firm, 12 to 13 minutes.

8 Keeping them on the baking mats on the baking sheets, let the cookies cool completely to room temperature.

9 Roll them in confectioners' sugar before serving.

(recipe continues)

VARIATIONS

Instead of confectioners' sugar, try topping them with German Buttercream (page 52) or White Chocolate Ganache Filling (page 42).

NOTES

To freeze the dough for later use, portion into balls as directed in step 5 and freeze in an airtight container for up to 3 months. Bake from frozen, increasing bake time by 1 more minute if necessary.

In an airtight container, the finished cookies will stay fresh at room temperature for up to 2 weeks. They also freeze well for up to 3 months. Thaw overnight in the fridge and then bring to room temperature before rolling in confectioners' sugar and serving.

Matcha Black Sesame Cookies

To share my treats, I used to do pop-up shops every few months. Those events allowed me to meet a lot of fellow bakers. Joe Luna ran a successful Swedish bun operation and had pop-ups around Sacramento almost weekly. Occasionally, he offered these cookies, which hooked me after just one bite! The matcha makes them taste earthy with a hint of bitterness, while the toasted sesame seeds make them chewy and fragrant—an incredible combination of textures and flavors.

PREP TIME: 15 minutes
COOK TIME: 15 minutes, plus resting and cooling time
TOTAL TIME: 1 hour 20 minutes
MAKES: 12 large cookies
OCCASIONS: Chinese New Year, Mid-Autumn Festival

175 grams (¾ cup) salted butter

200 grams (1 packed cup) brown sugar

75 grams (⅓ cup plus 1 tablespoon) granulated white sugar

1 teaspoon vanilla extract

½ teaspoon almond extract

1 egg, plus 1 yolk

½ teaspoon baking soda

10 grams (1½ tablespoons) matcha

10 chocolate sandwich cookies

200 grams (1⅓ cups) all-purpose flour

120 grams (1 cup) toasted black sesame seeds, plus more for garnish

White chocolate drizzle (optional)

1. In a microwave-safe dish, melt the butter by microwaving it on high for 20 to 30 seconds.

2. In a large mixing bowl, use a large wooden spoon or whisk to mix the sugars, melted butter, and extracts until well combined. The result will look like caramel.

3. Add the egg and yolk, baking soda, and matcha and stir to combine.

4. In a plastic storage bag, crush the sandwich cookies with a heavy mug or glass. Sift the flour.

5. Add the crushed cookies, sifted flour, and sesame seeds to the batter and mix until just combined. Don't overmix.

6. Cover and let rest on the counter for 30 minutes.

7. When ready to bake, preheat the oven to 325°F (163°C) and line a cookie sheet with a silicone mat.

8. Divide the dough into 12 equal portions and form them into the shape of hockey pucks.

9. Place six pucks per cookie sheet, giving them plenty of room to spread.

10. Bake until the middles have risen and slightly cracked, about 15 minutes, rotating halfway through.

11. On the baking sheets, let them cool completely to room temperature.

12. Drizzle with white chocolate if desired and garnish with additional black sesame seeds.

(recipe continues)

NOTES

Joe Luna gave me his blessing to share this recipe with you.

When you remove the cookies from the oven, they will feel *very* soft, which is OK!

Matcha makes them dry out quickly, so store them in an airtight container and enjoy them within a few days. If they harden, add a small piece of bread to the storage container for moisture.

Frozen in an airtight container, the cookies will stay fresh for up to 2 months.

Five-Spice Cookie Bars

In Chinese cooking, cinnamon primarily flavors savory dishes, such as braises, stir-fries, and stews, and of course it forms part of five-spice powder. Churros and cinnamon rolls introduced me to cinnamon sweets in America, and core-memory smells from the Cinnabon at the mall always make me feel super nostalgic for middle school. Bake up your own cinnamon-scented memories with this recipe.

PREP TIME: 20 minutes
COOK TIME: 25 minutes, plus cooling time
TOTAL TIME: 1 hour 20 minutes
MAKES: 8 large or 16 small bars
OCCASIONS: book club, high tea, birthdays, Mid-Autumn Festival, Rosh Hashanah, Oktoberfest, Thanksgiving

FOR THE FILLING

60 grams (¼ cup) salted butter

65 grams (⅓ packed cup) dark brown sugar

1½ teaspoons ground cinnamon

½ teaspoon five-spice powder

FOR THE DOUGH

175 grams (¾ cup) salted butter, room temperature

150 grams (¾ cup) granulated white sugar

1 large egg, room temperature

2 teaspoons vanilla extract

45 grams (3 tablespoons) heavy cream

1 teaspoon baking powder

½ teaspoon kosher salt

300 grams (2 cups) all-purpose flour

Neutral nonstick cooking spray

1   For the filling: Preheat the oven to 350°F (177°C) and, in a small microwave-safe bowl, melt the butter by microwaving it on high for approximately 30 seconds.

2   Stir in the brown sugar, cinnamon, and five-spice powder and set the filling aside.

3   For the dough: In the bowl of a stand mixer fitted with the paddle attachment, cream the butter and the granulated sugar on medium speed, until light and fluffy, for 2 minutes.

4   Add the egg, vanilla extract, heavy cream, baking powder, and salt. Continue to mix for 1 more minute, scraping the sides of the bowl as necessary.

5   Reduce the mixer speed to low, add the flour, and mix until just combined.

6   Divide the dough into three equal portions.

7   Spray an 8-by-8-by-2-inch baking dish with the cooking spray.

8   Press one portion of the dough into the dish and drizzle one-third of the filling onto it.

9   Repeat the process twice more.

10 Bake until the edges begin to brown, about 25 minutes.

11 In the pan, let cool completely to room temperature.

12 Flip the cookie block from the pan and top with the cream cheese frosting.

13 Slice into 8 or 16 bars.

(recipe continues)

1½ cups Cream Cheese Filling (page 39)

NOTE

In an airtight container, frosted cookie bars will stay fresh in the fridge for up to 1 week or frozen for up to 3 months.

VARIATIONS

For an ultra-gooey version, add chopped pieces of Microwave Mochi (page 146) before baking. If you don't like 5-spice, try this with just cinnamon—it's incredible! Enjoy this treat warm by skipping step 11.

Strawberry Shortcake Mochi Cookies

Every summer, my middle school sold strawberry shortcake ice cream bars at lunch, and occasionally I splurged on one. These cookie treats hide an Asian influence inside American nostalgia, and they're lots of fun to pull apart.

PREP TIME: 20 minutes

COOK TIME: 30 minutes, plus cooling time

TOTAL TIME: 2 hours

MAKES: 12 large cookies

OCCASIONS: girls' night, bake sales, picnics, Valentine's Day, Hanami, Mother's Day, bridal showers, baby showers

FOR THE STRAWBERRY CRUMBLE TOPPING

85 grams (3 ounces) dry strawberry gelatin powder

150 grams (1 cup) all-purpose flour

225 grams (1 cup) salted butter, room temperature

85 grams (3 ounces) dry vanilla pudding powder

FOR THE COOKIES

225 grams (1 cup) salted butter, room temperature

200 grams (1 packed cup) brown sugar

2 eggs, room temperature

2 teaspoons vanilla extract

½ teaspoon baking powder

¼ teaspoon baking soda

300 grams (2 cups) all-purpose flour

3 cups Microwave Mochi (page 146)

1. First make the topping. Preheat the oven to 350°F (177°C).

2. In a medium mixing bowl, add the strawberry gelatin, half the flour, and half the butter. Smash the butter with a fork and finish mixing by hand to combine to the consistency of sand that sticks to itself. Try not to melt the butter.

3. In another medium mixing bowl, repeat with the vanilla pudding powder and the rest of the flour and butter.

4. Line a cookie sheet with parchment paper or a silicone baking mat, pour both topping mixtures onto it, coarsely combine the two, and spread the mixture out into an even layer. Some chunks should remain for a crumbly texture.

5. Bake until the topping browns, 7 to 10 minutes, ensuring that it doesn't burn.

6. Remove from the oven, keep the oven on, and let the topping cool on the cookie sheet for 30 minutes.

7. After the topping has mostly cooled, make the cookies. In the bowl of a stand mixer fitted with the paddle attachment, cream the butter and sugar on medium speed until light and fluffy, about 3 minutes.

8. Add the eggs and vanilla extract and continue beating to combine, about 2 minutes.

9. Add the baking powder and baking soda and continue beating for 1 more minute to incorporate.

10. Add the flour and 1 cup of the strawberry crumble topping and mix on low until the dough just comes together, about 2 minutes.

11. Divide the dough into 12 equal portions.

12. Shape each portion into a disc, each about 4 to 5 inches in diameter.

(recipe continues)

VARIATIONS

You can adapt this recipe with lots of flavor modifications. For Vanilla Five-Spice Mochi Cookies, replace the strawberry gelatin with vanilla gelatin and the Strawberry Crumble Topping with Five-Spice Crumble Topping (page 11) and add 1 teaspoon of ground cinnamon in step 3.

Use any combination of gelatin and pudding that appeals to you, such as orange plus chocolate, raspberry plus pistachio, or key lime plus vanilla.

13 In the center of each disc, place ¼ cup of microwave mochi and wrap the dough up and around it, leaving no gaps.

14 Press the tops of the cookies in more strawberry crumble topping and place the cookies, topping sides up, on cookie sheets lined with baking mats (see Notes).

15 Bake until lightly golden brown, 12 to 15 minutes.

16 Remove from the oven, turn it off, and let the cookies cool completely to room temperature on the baking mats on the cookie sheets.

NOTES

In step 13, gaps aren't a dealbreaker, but the mochi will leak from them!

The Strawberry Crumble Topping adapts a recipe from Tracie's Place YouTube channel.

In an airtight container, store extra topping crumbles for up to 2 weeks or frozen for up to 3 months.

In an airtight container, the cookies will stay fresh at room temperature for up to 3 days, a week in the fridge, and frozen for up to 1 month.

Amaranth Sea Salt Chocolate Chip Cookies

In an Asian household, one of the best cooking compliments a baker can receive is: "Tastes good, not too sweet." This phrase inspired me to create this version of the classic American cookie for my family. Amaranth flour imparts a nutty flavor to baked goods, but it literally tastes like dirt to some people. If you substitute the amaranth flour for all-purpose flour (using only all-purpose for the recipe), you reduce a lot of this cookie's texture, chew, and shelf life, so baker beware!

PREP TIME: 20 minutes

COOK TIME: 13 minutes, plus resting and cooling time

TOTAL TIME: 1 day 1 hour

MAKES: 12 large cookies

OCCASIONS: dinner parties, bake sales, cookouts, picnics

---

115 grams (½ cup) salted butter, room temperature

150 grams (¾ packed cup) dark brown sugar

150 grams (¾ cup) Miss Jones Baking Co. SmartSugar

1 teaspoon baking soda

1 teaspoon baking powder

2 large eggs, room temperature

1½ teaspoons vanilla extract

225 grams (1½ cups) all-purpose flour

100 grams (⅔ cup) amaranth flour

350 grams (2¼ cups) chocolate chips, plus more if desired

Coarse sea salt for sprinkling

1 In a stand mixer fitted with the paddle attachment, cream the butter, both sugars, baking soda, and baking powder on medium until the mixture resembles coarse sand, about 3 minutes.

2 Add the eggs and vanilla, increase the speed to high, and beat to combine until the mixtures lightens and becomes fluffy, about 2 minutes.

3 All at once, add both flours and the chocolate chips. Decrease the speed to low and mix until the dough just comes together, about 1 minute. Don't overmix.

4 Using a ¼-cup cookie scoop or measuring cup, scoop the dough into 12 equal portions and roll each into a ball.

5 Into the tops of the dough balls, press extra chocolate chips if desired and sprinkle with sea salt.

6 Cover cookie dough balls with plastic wrap and refrigerate for 24 hours before baking.

7 When ready to bake, preheat the oven to 350°F (177°C) and line cookie sheets with baking mats. Place 6 cookies per baking sheet, leaving even space between them so they can spread.

8 Bake until the centers set and the edges turn slightly golden brown, 12 to 14 minutes. Halfway through, rotate the sheets and use the bottom of a plate to smash the cookies down to about ½ inch thick.

9 On the cookie sheets, let the cookies cool for 20 minutes before serving.

(recipe continues)

TIPS: Texture will vary based on baking time, storage method, and cookie freshness. Freshly baked cookies run crisp around the edges and melty in the center. Letting them sit, uncovered, for 1 day results in firmer chocolate chips and different textures on the edges and in the centers of the cookies.

NOTES

In step 3, overmixing can result in tough cookies. Before resting, ensure the dough balls don't contain any air pockets.

In an airtight container on the counter or in the fridge, the cookies will become homogeneously soft and chewy, and stay fresh for up to 1 week.

VARIATION

If you can't find the Miss Jones Baking Co. SmartSugar, use the same amount of coconut sugar.

If you like this cookie's texture but want to a totally different flavor, modify the add-ins: white chocolate, dried cranberries, and macadmia nuts are a classic twist.

Dark Chocolate Passion Fruit Cookies

For my birthday a few years ago, a friend sent me brownies from a cottage baker who used fruit-flavored chocolate medallions (known as fèves) in them for a burst of tartness. They blew my mind and set me on a mission to incorporate them into my cookies. Use passion fruit fèves to baseline how they should taste. But baker beware: Commercial fèves cost a lot. Instead, you can make your own fèves by tempering white chocolate with freeze-dried passion fruit powder.

PREP TIME: 15 minutes

COOK TIME: 14 minutes, plus resting and cooling time

TOTAL TIME: 1 day 1 hour

MAKES: 12 large cookies

OCCASIONS: dinner parties, book club, girls' night, bake sales, high tea, Valentine's Day, Easter, Mother's Day, bridal showers

---

200 grams (1⅓ cups) all-purpose flour

60 grams (½ cup) bread flour

115 grams (1½ cups) dark cocoa powder

1 teaspoon cornstarch

½ teaspoon baking soda

115 grams (½ cup) salted butter, room temperature

100 grams (½ packed cup) brown sugar

75 grams (⅓ cup plus 1 tablespoon) granulated white sugar

85 grams (3 ounces) dark chocolate of choice

85 grams (3 ounces) passion fruit fèves

1 large egg, plus 1 large yolk, room temperature

1 teaspoon vanilla extract

Coarse sea salt for sprinkling

1 In a medium mixing bowl, sift together the flours, cocoa powder, cornstarch, and baking soda.

2 In a bowl of a stand mixer fitted with the paddle attachment, cream the butter and sugars on medium until light and fluffy, 6 to 7 minutes.

3 While the butter is creaming, rough-chop the dark chocolate and break the fèves into halves, reserving 12 whole fèves. Set both aside.

4 To the creamed butter, add the egg and yolk and continue to mix for 3 minutes to combine, scraping down the sides of the bowl as needed.

5 Add the vanilla extract and continue mixing for 1 more minute.

6 All at once, add the dry ingredients and mix on low to combine, about 2 minutes. No flour streaks should remain.

7 With a rubber or silicone spatula, gently stir in the chopped chocolate and halved passion fruit fèves.

8 Divide the dough into 12 equal portions and roll each into a ball.

9 Into the top of each dough ball, press 1 whole fève and sprinkle with coarse sea salt.

10 Cover the dough balls with plastic wrap or place them in an airtight container and refrigerate for 24 hours.

11 When ready to bake, preheat the oven to 350°F (177°C) and line two cookie sheets with baking mats.

12 Place the dough balls on the mats, 6 to a cookie sheet, evenly spaced.

(recipe continues)

13   Bake until the cookies set, 12 to 14 minutes.

14   Keeping them on the baking mats on the cookie sheets, let the cookies cool completely to room temperature, about 30 minutes.

NOTES

Formed dough balls will keep in the freezer for up to 6 months. When frozen for a long time, they lose a lot of moisture. The longer you freeze them, the more domed they'll appear after baking.

If you prefer a flatter look, press the dough down halfway through the bake.

The recipe as-is creates very soft, fudgey cookies. If you want a more firm cookie, increase flour by 50 grams, or $^{1}/_{3}$ cup.

In an airtight container, baked cookies will stay fresh for up to 1 week in the fridge and frozen for up to 3 months.

VARIATION

Instead of buying fèves, you can make you own by tempering white chocolate with passion fruit powder (or other fat-soluble flavors of your choosing, such as matcha powder, coconut powder, or another chocolate-friendly option). Rough-chop 150 grams (5 ounces) of white chocolate and melt it in a double boiler on low heat. When the chocolate runs smooth, stir in the powder. Start with 10 grams (⅓ ounce) of powder and increase to taste. Allow to cool for a few minutes, then pour into a piping bag and pipe little discs of flavored chocolate about the size of a dime. Allow to cool fully and store in an airtight container at room temperature or in the fridge for up to 6 months.

5

Cookie Combinations and Boba- Inspired Bakes

For my first "real" job, I worked as a barista in a Bay Area boba shop, making drinks and tending the register. After learning the basics, I started experimenting with flavor combinations. These recipes honor that experience and the people there who encouraged me.

THE BOBA BEGINNINGS OF BORDERLANDS BAKERY

At the boba shop I worked at in Union City, I always sought the fastest, most efficient ways to do my work. Customers often were digging for money *after* I had made their drinks. The compliments about my speed made me thrive. The job paid a little more than minimum wage, but I couldn't have been happier.

The couple who owned the store noticed my efficiency. If I had wanted it, they would have promoted me to store manager, and my life today would look very different. They gave me the freedom to explore the best ways to do the work while also encouraging me to pursue side hustles and a college degree. While working part time there, I was making jewelry to sell it online and importing Asian skincare products for resale. When business in the boba shop was slow, the owners didn't mind if I spent time on other activities.

That shop gave me my first taste of working in the "real" world. It taught me the basics of managing time, being accountable, and following through. It never felt like work. The couple had young kids, and the wife, my boss, ran a few small businesses. The husband worked as a field service engineer for a biotech company and occasionally helped with the family enterprises. They taught me about owning and operating businesses professionally and navigating life as part of a couple. They saw potential in me and encouraged me to chase what I loved, sowing the seeds that later helped me create and grow Borderlands Bakery.

Mango Coconut Cookies

Growing up, I hated coconut—maybe because my parents insisted that I was crazy not to like the flavor, which only made me hate it more. We rarely ate mango, but I developed a taste for it later in life. According to traditional Chinese herbology (page 126), this recipe beneficially combines a hot food (mango) and a cold food (coconut). The fact that I love these cookies probably will make my parents laugh. They tried *so* hard to get me to eat a balanced diet as a kid. To celebrate the publication of this book, I'm going to make them this recipe and thank them.

PREP TIME: 20 minutes

COOK TIME: 15 minutes, plus cooling time

TOTAL TIME: 1 hour

MAKES: 24 cookies (3-inch diameter)

OCCASIONS: Potluck, bake sales, high tea, picnics, cookouts, hiking, road trips

---

75 grams (½ cup) dried mangoes

1 lime

225 grams (1 cup) salted butter, room temperature

150 grams (¾ cup) coconut sugar

1 teaspoon vanilla extract

1 large egg

250 grams (1⅔ cups) all-purpose flour

75 grams (¾ cup) sweetened shredded coconut

TIPS: If you can, buy dried mangoes with no sugar added, which will result in a more balanced cookie flavor.

1 Preheat the oven to 350°F (177°C) and line two cookie sheets with parchment paper.

2 Finely chop the mangoes and zest the lime.

3 In the bowl of a stand mixer fitted with the paddle attachment, cream the butter, sugar, vanilla extract, and lime zest on medium until light and fluffy, about 2 minutes.

4 Add the egg and continue beating for 2 minutes to mix well.

5 Add half of the flour and mix until just incorporated before adding the second half, about 3 minutes total.

6 Add the coconut and mangoes and continue mixing for 2 minutes to combine. Don't overmix.

7 Onto a flat surface, turn out the mixture and divide it into 24 equal portions and roll them into balls.

8 Bake until the cookies turn lightly golden, 12 to 14 minutes.

9 Remove from the oven and let them cool on the sheets for 10 minutes before transferring to a wire rack to cool completely to room temperature.

NOTES

This dough keeps well and, in an airtight container, stays fresh when portioned and frozen for up to 3 months. In an airtight container, baked cookies will stay fresh at room temperature for 3 days or frozen for up to 1 month.

VARIATIONS

Ginger and coconut make a great pairing. For Ginger Coconut Cookies, replace the dried mangoes with 50 grams (¼ cup) of candied ginger.

THE FOUR NATURES

Traditional Chinese herbology posits four natures: hot, warm, (neutral), cool, and cold. Those designations have nothing to do with the temperatures of the foods. The idea behind the system holds that we should eat a diet that balances hot and cold foods to help manage our health. Hot foods include red meat, oily foods, onions, garlic, ginger, and mangoes. Cool foods include coconuts, most fruits, leafy greens, most fish, and grains. Pork, duck, potatoes, and mushrooms, among other foods, count as neutral. For thousands of years, people have practiced and developed Chinese herbology, one area of traditional Chinese medicine, but only recently have researchers begun to acknowledge, investigate, and understand the quantifiable science underlying these theories. As a teenager, I had a strong preference for hot-leaning foods, such as red meat, so my mom always tried to entice me to eat more cooling foods to help manage my stress and temper. I should have listened to her!

Milk Tea Boba Cookies

Made with black tea, tapioca pearls, milk or creamer, and sugar, boba milk tea originated in Taiwan in the 1980s. It caught on in Asian communities in California in the 1990s, but only more recently has it become popular in the rest of the country. It's becoming so mainstream that lots of coffee shops offer tapioca pearls, standard, for cold tea beverages. Make this cookie recipe to enjoy the chewy texture of those pearls in a more satiating snack.

PREP TIME: 10 minutes
COOK TIME: 30 minutes, plus freezing and cooling time
TOTAL TIME: 1 hour 30 minutes
MAKES: 12 large cookies
OCCASIONS: Lunar New Year, potlucks, picnics, bake sales

175 grams (¾ cup) salted butter

180 grams (1 cup) uncooked (dry) tapioca pearls

40 grams (3 packed tablespoons) dark brown sugar for the bobas, plus 150 grams (¾ packed cup) for the dough

75 grams (⅓ cup) instant milk tea powder

100 grams (½ cup) granulated white sugar

½ teaspoon baking powder

½ teaspoon baking soda

½ teaspoon salt

1 egg, plus 1 yolk

300 grams (2 cups) all-purpose flour

1   In a microwave-safe bowl, microwave the butter on high for 30 seconds to melt it, then let it cool to room temperature while you make the bobas.

2   In a medium saucepan over high heat, bring 4 cups of water to a rolling boil.

3   With a large slotted spoon, add the tapioca pearls to the boiling water and stir to prevent them from sticking to the bottom.

4   Reduce heat to low and simmer, stirring occasionally, until the bobas cook through and become chewy but not mushy, 12 to 15 minutes.

5   While the pearls are cooking, add the 40 grams of dark brown sugar to a small bowl.

6   When the bobas finish cooking, drain and stir them immediately into the 40 grams of brown sugar to cool. Set aside and resist the urge to eat them all.

7   In a large mixing bowl, stir together the milk tea powder, remaining 150 grams dark brown sugar, white sugar, baking powder, baking soda, and salt.

8   Add the cooled butter and mix to combine.

9   Add the egg and yolk and mix until you achieve a grainy base like caramel.

10 Sift in the flour and mix to combine almost all the way.

11 Before incorporating all the flour, gently stir in the bobas and finish mixing.

12 Divide the dough into 12 equal portions, roll them into balls, press them into the shape of hockey pucks, and place the pucks on baking mats on two cookie sheets, 6 cookies per sheet.

(recipe continues)

VARIATIONS

Instead of dark brown sugar, you can mix your boiled bobas in honey. Also try adding some crumble (page 11) on the top to create another layer of texture.

You can substitute the milk tea powder with other flavored drink powders (honeydew, pandan, strawberry, Thai tea, and more) for a totally different cookie!

13 Cover with plastic wrap and freeze for 20 minutes or until you're ready to bake.

14 When ready to bake, preheat the oven to 350°F (177°C).

15 From frozen, bake just until the cookies start to puff in the middle, 13 to 16 minutes.

16 Remove from the oven and, if desired, use a circle cookie cutter to adjust the shapes.

17 Let the cookies cool completely on the cookie sheets.

NOTES

Freezing the dough preserves the texture of the tapioca pearls before baking.

After baking, boba balls harden quickly and don't keep well, so enjoy the cookies the same day you bake them.

Strawberry Sugar Cookies with Matcha Coconut Milk Spread

A matcha strawberry drink created by the Boba Guys shop inspired these cookies, which taste sweet, fruity, earthy, and decadent all at the same time. On TikTok, a woman eating fresh strawberries with matcha spread introduced me to the topping. She had bought her jar from Japan. You can find matcha spread on Amazon, but it can cost a lot. Instead, you can make your own vegan version.

PREP TIME: 20 minutes

COOK TIME: 30 minutes, plus cooling time

TOTAL TIME: 1 hour 30 minutes

MAKES: 12 jumbo cookies

OCCASIONS: Lunar New Year, Christmas, picnics

FOR THE MATCHA COCONUT MILK SPREAD

60 grams (¼ cup) water

2 teaspoons matcha

3 teaspoons granulated white sugar

1 teaspoon cornstarch

240 grams (1 cup) coconut milk

FOR THE STRAWBERRY SUGAR COOKIES

100 grams (3 cups) freeze-dried strawberries, plus more for garnish

225 grams (1 cup) salted butter, room temperature

200 grams (1 cup) granulated white sugar

2 teaspoons vanilla extract

1 large egg

250 grams (1⅔ cups) all-purpose flour

1 teaspoon baking soda

100 grams (⅓ cup) strawberry jam

1. First make the matcha coconut milk spread. In a kettle or microwave, boil the water.

2. Sift the matcha into a heat-safe jar or bowl and add the boiled water.

3. Stir in the sugar and cornstarch and mix until they dissolve completely.

4. In a small saucepan over medium-low heat, bring the coconut milk to a simmer.

5. While whisking, gradually pour the matcha mixture through a sieve into the simmering milk.

6. Cook, whisking occasionally, until the mixture reduces by half, thickens, and becomes smooth and creamy, about 20 minutes (see Notes).

7. While the matcha coconut milk spread is cooking, start making the strawberry sugar cookies. Preheat the oven to 350°F (177°C) and line two baking or cookie sheets with parchment paper or silicone baking mats.

8. In a blender or food processor, pulverize the freeze-dried strawberries to a fine powder.

9. In the bowl of a stand mixer fitted with the paddle attachment, cream the butter, sugar, and vanilla extract until light and fluffy, about 2 minutes.

10. Add the egg and continue mixing to combine, 2 more minutes.

11. Add the flour, baking soda, ¼ cup of the pulverized strawberries from step 8, and the strawberry jam and continue mixing to combine, about 90 seconds.

(recipe continues)

TIPS: Use high-quality matcha for best results. In step 5, if the sieve catches any lumps, spoon hot milk from the saucepan over them and push them through with the back of the spoon. The matcha milk spread also tastes amazing on toast and fresh fruit.

12 Using a 1-tablespoon ice cream scoop, melon baller, cookie scoop, or soup spoon, scoop the dough and roll into 12 balls. Place the balls on the prepared baking sheets, leaving 2 inches on all sides of each cookie.

13 Bake for 8 minutes, rotate the sheets, and continue baking until the edges just begin to set, 2 to 3 more minutes.

14 When the matcha coconut milk spread has finished cooking, remove it from the heat and let it cool to room temperature.

15 When the strawberry sugar cookies have finished cooking, remove from the oven and let them cool on the baking sheets. They will continue to cook a little as they cool.

16 After the cookies have cooled, slather them with a generous layer of matcha coconut milk spread and garnish with the remaining freeze-dried strawberries.

NOTES

The matcha coconut milk spread has finished cooking if, when you run a spoon or whisk across the bottom of the saucepan, it leaves a line that doesn't close. If you scrape the pan but you can't see a line, continue whisking and cooking. The spread will thicken after cooling.

Store extra matcha milk spread in an airtight container in the fridge up for up to 1 week or in the freezer for up to 2 months.

VARIATION

You can also make the matcha milk spread with cow's milk, if desired, instead of coconut milk.

Peach Green Tea Gummies

One year, a friend spoiled me with Sugarfina candies, and the product design—beautiful boxes containing playful flavors of gummy candies—seriously impressed me. Those candies inspired me to turn one of my favorite green tea flavors into this yummy gummy.

PREP TIME: 25 minutes

COOK TIME: 10 minutes, plus cooling time

TOTAL TIME: 2 hours 30 minutes

MAKES: 36 gummies

OCCASIONS: New Year's Eve, Valentine's Day, picnics, bachelor/ette parties, bridal showers

---

Neutral oil (such as canola or vegetable oil) for greasing

120 grams (½ cup) water

60 grams (½ cup) green tea, loose

300 grams (1½ cups) peach puree

300 grams (1½ cups) granulated white sugar

30 grams (2 tablespoons) fresh lemon juice

100 grams (⅓ cup) corn syrup

12 grams (1½ tablespoons) unflavored gelatin powder

1 Spray molds of choice or a shallow baking dish with oil.

2 In a medium saucepan over medium heat, heat the water until hot but not boiling, about 3 minutes.

3 Remove from heat, add the tea, and steep for 10 minutes.

4 Strain out the tea and discard the leaves. Return the liquid to the saucepan.

5 Add the peach puree, sugar, lemon juice, and corn syrup and stir constantly over medium heat until the sugar dissolves completely.

6 Whisk the gelatin powder into the liquid until fully incorporated.

7 Continue stirring until the mixture boils.

8 Remove from heat and let the mixture cool for 2 minutes.

9 Pour the liquid into the prepared molds or baking dish.

10 Let the molded gummies or gummy block sit at room temperature until fully set, about 2 hours.

11 After the gummies have set, remove from the molds or baking dish. If using a dish, slice into shapes of choice.

VARIATIONS

After the gummies have set, roll them in granulated white sugar or citric acid powder for some nice tang. You also can heat-seal them, along with a pinch of cornstarch, in cellophane or polyethylene baggies.

NOTES

If peach puree is difficult to find, pulse canned peaches (juice and all) in a food processor or blender until it's a uniform puree. In an airtight container, store the gummies at room temperature for up to 2 weeks. If you don't store them in a cool, dry place, they'll melt into a sad, goopy mess!

Peach Green Tea Gummies

Vietnamese Coffee Pavlova

Vietnamese Coffee Pavlova

Named after a Russian prima ballerina, pavlovas originated either in Australia or New Zealand at the start of the 1900s. Whipped cream and fruit traditionally top meringue in the shape of a nest or bowl, but many countries have adapted it. In America, meringue cookies, crisp throughout, usually come no larger than a cracker. Pavlovas usually don't bake all the way through, resulting in a crisp, meringue shell with a softer, chewier center. In Venice, which I visited in 2017 and 2019, bakery windows displayed giant pavlovas in all colors, and *pasticceri* (pastry chefs) flavored the incredibly satisfying meringue with various jams. This recipe creates a pavlova "cake" that honors java lovers who want another delicious way to enjoy Vietnamese coffee.

PREP TIME: 15 minutes

COOK TIME: 1 hour 10 minutes, plus cooling time

TOTAL TIME: 4 hours

SERVES: 8

OCCASIONS: birthdays, anniversaries, bridal showers, high tea, book club

FOR THE PAVLOVAS

4 egg whites

1 teaspoon cornstarch

1 pinch cream of tartar

150 grams (¾ cups) granulated white sugar

1 teaspoon vanilla bean paste

1 teaspoon instant coffee

FOR THE COFFEE SYRUP

125 grams (½ cup) prepared Vietnamese coffee (plain black)

50 grams (¼ packed cup) brown sugar

Condensed milk for drizzling

Whipped cream (optional)

1   Preheat the oven to 350°F (177°C).

2   In the bowl of a stand mixer fitted with the whisk attachment, beat the egg whites on medium until frothy, about 3 minutes. While beating, add the cornstarch and cream of tartar.

3   Add the white sugar, 1 tablespoon at a time, until it completely dissolves, the meringue has become glossy, and stiff peaks form, about 5 to 8 minutes.

4   Add the vanilla bean paste and instant coffee and continue beating until combined.

5   Line a baking sheet with a silicone baking mat and, using a spatula, divide the meringue into two equal "cakes."

6   Bake for 10 minutes to quick-set their shape.

7   Reduce the heat to 200°F (93°C) and bake for 1 hour (see Tips).

8   Turn off the oven, keeping the pavlovas inside, and let them cool for 2 hours.

9   While the pavlovas are cooling, make the coffee syrup. In a small saucepan over medium heat, combine the Vietnamese coffee and brown sugar and cook, stirring constantly until a thick syrup forms, about 5 minutes.

10   Remove from the heat and allow to cool to room temperature.

TIPS: In step 7, rotate the baking sheet halfway through *only* if you notice uneven browning. Opening the oven door lets out a lot of heat, and you want to prevent heat loss during the bake.

11 When the pavlovas have cooled, place one on a serving platter and drizzle it with half the coffee syrup and condensed milk to taste.

12 Place the second pavlova on top, pressing down very gently. Top with the rest of the coffee syrup, condensed milk, and whipped cream if desired, and serve.

NOTES

When baking the pavlovas for 10 minutes to quick-set their shape, it's OK if they brown a little.

You don't have to stack the finished pavlovas, but doing so creates a beautiful presentation.

Pavlovas don't freeze well, so enjoy them right away.

VARIATION

Instead of Vietnamese coffee, you can use 2 shots of espresso diluted with enough water to create ½ cup of liquid.

Thai Milk Tea Cream Puffs

Working in a boba shop as a teen developed my palate for milk tea beverages. Everyone has different flavor preferences, but in my professional opinion, the tea (flavor) needs to taste strong, the milk or creamer shouldn't overpower it, and the sweetness shouldn't overwhelm the overall drink. On a visit to Paris in 2022, I took a choux pastry class, which inspired me to create these cream puffs that incorporate flavors from my youth.

PREP TIME: 30 minutes

COOK TIME: 30 minutes, plus cooling and setting time

TOTAL TIME: 4 hours

MAKES: 12 cream puffs

OCCASIONS: High tea, picnics, bridal showers, baby showers, Chinese New Year, potlucks

FOR THE CRAQUELIN

50 grams (3½ tablespoons) salted butter, room temperature

65 grams (⅓ packed cup) brown sugar

75 grams (½ cup) all-purpose flour

FOR THE PASTRY CREAM

500 grams (2 cups) whole milk

25 grams (6 tablespoons) instant Thai tea mix

30 grams (2 tablespoons) salted butter

4 egg yolks

100 grams (½ cup) granulated white sugar

30 grams (¼ cup) cornstarch

1   First, make the craquelin. In the bowl of a stand mixer fitted with the paddle attachment, beat the butter, brown sugar, and flour on medium until the dough just comes together, about 4 minutes.

2   Turn out the dough onto a sheet of parchment paper or plastic wrap and roll it to 1 or 2 millimeters thick (see Tips).

3   Top the dough with another sheet of parchment paper or plastic wrap to prevent it from drying, and freeze it until ready to bake.

4   Next, make the pastry cream. In a medium saucepan over medium heat, bring the milk to a boil, stirring often.

5   When it boils, remove from the heat, add the Thai tea mix, and whisk until the powder dissolves.

6   Stir in the butter until incorporated into the pastry cream.

7   Let the hot milk tea mix cool for 30 minutes.

8   After the milk tea has cooled, whisk in the egg yolks until smooth.

9   Over medium heat, return the saucepan to the stove, add the white sugar and cornstarch, and bring the custard to a boil, whisking constantly to prevent burning.

10 When the custard boils, turn off the heat and whisk vigorously until it thickens, about 2 minutes.

11 Through a sieve, strain the hot custard to remove any chunks.

12 Pour the hot custard into a piping bag and seal the top, leaving no air at the top of the bag. Refrigerate for at least 2 hours to set before using.

(recipe continues)

FOR THE CHOUX PASTRY

75 grams (½ cup) all-purpose flour

60 grams (¼ cup) whole milk

50 grams (3½ tablespoons) salted butter

1 teaspoon granulated white sugar

60 grams (¼ cup) water

2 large eggs, room temperature

NOTE

When baking the choux pastry in steps 21 and 22, *don't* open the oven door, which will cause the choux to deflate.

VARIATION

Take your cream puffs to the next level by topping them with a swirl of German Buttercream (page 52) and a boba pearl or three.

---

13 While the pastry cream is setting, make the choux. Preheat the oven to 425°F (218°C). Sift the flour.

14 In a saucepan over medium heat, bring the milk, butter, white sugar, and water to a boil.

15 Turn off the heat, but don't remove the saucepan from the stove. Add the flour all at once and stir vigorously with a spatula to create a thick and smooth dough.

16 Transfer the dough to the bowl of a stand mixer fitted with the paddle attachment and beat on medium to release steam and cool the dough, about 2 minutes. The dough should feel warm but not hot.

17 Add 1 of the eggs and continue beating to combine fully before repeating with the second egg. The dough should have loosened to the consistency of thick paste.

18 Transfer the dough to a piping bag with a large round tip or a tipless piping bag trimmed to 1 centimeter (½ inch) wide.

19 Pipe into 12 small mounds, approximately 1½ inches in diameter, onto a baking mat on a cookie sheet.

20 From the freezer, remove the frozen craquelin and use a circle cutter to cut out 12 circles that are the size of the piped mounds in step 19. Place each atop one of the raw pastry mounds.

21 Bake until the choux have puffed but not browned, about 12 minutes.

22 Reduce the temperature to 350°F (177°C) and bake until golden brown, about 8 more minutes.

23 Turn off the oven and, still inside, let the choux cool for 30 minutes. After removing them from the oven, let them rest at room temperature.

24 With the piping bag, puncture the bottoms of the choux, pipe the pastry cream into them, and serve immediately.

TIPS: In step 2, to avoid having flimsy dough, roll the craquelin dough on the bottom of a cookie sheet, cover it, and transfer as is to the freezer. In step 15, you want to dry the dough a bit, so keep the pan on the stove so that the residual heat evaporates some of the moisture. For the crisp craquelin to contrast with the smooth pastry cream, eat the cream puffs as soon as you finish making them.

Honey Lemon Ginger Pâte de Fruit

Hong Kongers drink lots of honey lemon tea, which I've enjoyed in Hong Kong–style cafés. Wanting to capture those nostalgic flavors led me to encapsulate them in this jelly candy. At a local pop-up, Nariya Charoensupaya, a super talented pastry chef with a cottage bakery, introduced me to pâte de fruit: delicious cubes of firm fruit jelly rolled in sugar. Imagine the crunchiness of the granulated sugar wrapped around a smooth, soft, concentrated jelly (not gummy) explosion of fruity flavors. They're so much fun to eat.

PREP TIME: 5 minutes

COOK TIME: 15 minutes, plus cooling and setting time

TOTAL TIME: 8 hours 30 minutes

MAKES: 36 pieces

OCCASIONS: picnics, cookouts, Lunar New Year

---

10 grams (1 tablespoon) fresh ginger, peeled

200 grams (¾ cup) honey

300 grams (1½ cups) granulated white sugar, plus more for coating

120 grams (½ cup) fresh lemon juice

15 grams (1 tablespoon) lemon zest

Vegetable or canola oil for greasing

15 grams (1 tablespoon) powdered pectin

1 Finely grate the ginger.

2 In a medium saucepan over medium-high heat, combine the honey, sugar, lemon juice, lemon zest, and grated ginger, stirring occasionally, until the mixture reaches 225°F (107°C) on a candy thermometer.

3 While the mixture is heating, grease an 8-by-8-inch baking dish, line it with parchment paper, and grease the paper, as well.

4 Stir the powdered pectin into the honey mixture.

5 Bring the mixture to a boil and, stirring constantly, cook for 1 more minute to dissolve the pectin fully.

6 Remove from heat and pour the mixture into the prepared pan.

7 On the counter, let the mixture cool to room temperature for 1 hour, then cover and transfer to the fridge to set overnight.

8 After the mixture has set, flip it from the pan and cut it into 1⅓-inch squares or the shapes of your choice.

9 Toss the pieces in granulated sugar to coat.

(recipe continues)

NOTES

Every brand of honey is a little different and if the jelly won't set, add more pectin, 2 grams at a time, or cook the mixture until it reaches 235°F. In an airtight container at room temperature, pâte de fruit keeps well for weeks. Over longer spans of time, the pieces will dry out, resulting in a thicker sugar shell, which you may like!

VARIATIONS

In step 8, use mini cookie cutters to create fun shapes.

For Honey Lemon Rosemary Pâte de Fruit, replace the ginger with 10 grams (3 tablespoons) of rosemary in step 2 and remove it before step 4.

For Honey Lime Lemongrass Pâte de Fruit, replace the ginger with four 3-inch pieces of lemongrass, smashed, and remove before step 4. Replace the lemon zest with lime zest, and replace the lemon juice with 60 grams (¼ cup) of water and 60 grams (¼ cup) of lime juice.

6

Joyful Confections

In the baking world, people love to go crazy with flavor combinations and over-the-top decorations, but sometimes simplicity brings the most joy. This chapter contains simple recipes and a few elaborate dishes, all of them designed to bring you the same joy that they give me.

Microwave Mochi

For many non-Asian Americans, mochi ice cream serves as the gateway sweet to mochi. In addition to traditional treats and ice cream, you can find mochi in donuts, muffins, soup, waffles, yogurts, and other foods. This super-easy recipe makes mochi for a variety of applications. Roll it out and wrap it around ice cream, fresh fruit, or whipped cream and jams. Cut it into rectangles or tubes. Wrap bacon around it and grill for a sweet and savory snack. So many possibilities!

PREP TIME: 5 minutes
COOK TIME: 4 minutes, plus cooling time
TOTAL TIME: 25 minutes
MAKES: approximately 36 cubes (½ inch)
OCCASIONS: Lunar New Year, New Year's Eve

150 grams (1¼ cups) sweet rice flour (mochiko)

200 grams (1 cup) granulated white sugar

¼ teaspoon baking powder

1 teaspoon vanilla extract

240 grams (1 cup) water

Cornstarch or potato starch for dusting

1 In a large microwave-safe bowl, whisk together the mochiko, sugar, and baking powder.

2 Add the vanilla extract and the water and whisk until smooth and well combined.

3 Cover the bowl with plastic wrap, leaving a small vent, and microwave on high until the mixture cooks through, 2 to 3 minutes.

4 Leaving the plastic wrap on the bowl, let the mochi cool for 5 minutes.

5 Dust your hands with cornstarch and remove the mochi blob from the bowl.

6 Knead it until it becomes smooth and elastic, about 3 minutes.

7 Dust a flat surface with cornstarch and roll out the mochi to ½ inch thick or desired thickness.

8 Use a cookie cutter or knife to cut it into shapes.

> **NOTES**
> Mochi dries out quickly. Store it in an airtight container at room temperature for up to 2 days or in the freezer for up to 1 month.

VARIATIONS
Instead of furikake, try topping the muffins with sesame seeds and/or salt of choice, such as bacon salt, Maldon sea salt, smoked salt, or vanilla salt.

Chocolate Banana Mochi Mini Muffins with Furikake

The Boba Guys shop introduced me to mochi muffins. The first one I tried came full size. It tasted dense and chewy, with a crunchy crust that had softened while sitting in the display case in the store. This version, adapted from a Snixy Kitchen recipe, always pleases a crowd, regardless of cultural background. When fresh, the crispy crust gives way to a chewy interior, a nice study in contrast. Furikake, a Japanese roasted seaweed condiment, tempers the sweetness of the muffins. It's all about balance.

PREP TIME: 15 minutes
COOK TIME: 30 minutes, plus cooling time
TOTAL TIME: 1 hour
MAKES: 24 mini muffins
OCCASIONS: picnics, cookouts, road trips, hiking

60 grams (¼ cup) salted butter

1 teaspoon molasses

200 grams (1 packed cup) dark brown sugar

1 large egg, room temperature

370 grams (one 13-ounce can) coconut milk

1 teaspoon vanilla extract

85 grams (3 ounces) ripe banana

200 grams (1½ cups) sweet rice flour (mochiko)

2 teaspoons baking powder

½ teaspoon baking soda

100 grams (½ cup) chocolate chips

Toasted black and white sesame seeds for topping

Furikake for topping

1 In a large microwave-safe bowl, microwave the butter on high for 15 or 20 seconds to melt it, and let it cool to room temperature for 2 or 3 minutes.

2 Preheat the oven to 375°F (190°C) and line a muffin tin with paper liners.

3 Whisk the molasses and brown sugar into the melted butter until smooth.

4 Add the egg and mix to combine.

5 Stir in the coconut milk and vanilla extract until combined.

6 Mash the banana and mix to incorporate fully.

7 In a medium bowl, whisk together the mochiko, baking powder, and baking soda.

8 Gradually add the dry ingredients and chocolate chips to the wet ingredients, stirring until just combined.

9 Pour the batter evenly into the muffin liners and top with toasted sesame seeds and furikake to taste.

10 Bake until the tops turn a deep caramelized brown and a toothpick inserted into the center comes out clean, 25 to 30 minutes.

11 In the tin, let the muffins cool for 5 minutes, then transfer to a wire rack to cool completely.

> **NOTES**
>
> In an airtight container, store the muffins in the fridge for up to 1 week or in the freezer for 1 month. To get that crunch back, pop them in a toaster oven on medium for 5 minutes.

Hong Kong Sponge Cakes

When I was in high school, my parents took me to a Chinese bakery in San Francisco for special occasions. If we were lucky, they had these simple, small sponge cakes. With a great texture and not too sweet, they made for a perfect snack. They tasted like sponge cake with a subtle custard flavor, which I've modified with vanilla bean paste for some luxurious flair. Traditionally they bake in tulip baking cups—large, tall tins with dramatic liners resembling tulip petals or popped shirt collars, as pictured—but regular liners work just fine, too.

PREP TIME: 15 minutes
COOK TIME: 30 minutes, plus cooling time
TOTAL TIME: 1 hour
MAKES: 12 cupcakes
OCCASIONS: breakfast, snacks, hiking, birthdays

60 grams (¼ cup) salted butter
5 eggs
60 grams (¼ cup) whole milk
100 grams (⅔ cup) cake flour
¼ teaspoon vanilla bean paste
¼ teaspoon cream of tartar
65 grams (⅓ cup) granulated white sugar
Jam of choice for serving

VARIATION
Before baking, top the batter with slivered almonds for a little nutty flavor.

1 In a large microwave-safe bowl, microwave the butter on high for 30 seconds to melt it and set aside to cool; meanwhile, continue with the rest of the steps.

2 Preheat the oven to 350°F (177°C) and line a muffin tin with paper liners.

3 Separate the egg whites and yolks.

4 Add the milk to the melted butter, sift the cake flour into it, and mix well with a spatula.

5 Beat the egg yolks, add the yolks and vanilla bean paste to the mixture, and combine thoroughly.

6 In the bowl of a stand mixer fitted with the whisk attachment or using a hand mixer in a medium mixing bowl, beat the egg whites and cream of tartar on medium until big frothy bubbles form, about 1 minute.

7 Add the sugar to the egg whites and beat on high until very stiff peaks form, about 3 minutes.

8 With a spatula, gently fold one-third of the meringue into the batter until just incorporated.

9 Repeat twice more with the rest of the meringue.

10 Pour the batter equally into the cupcake liners.

11 Bake until a toothpick inserted into the center comes out clean, 25 to 30 minutes.

12 Let the cakes cool for 2 minutes in the tin, then transfer to a wire rack to cool completely.

13 Enjoy plain or serve with butter and/or your favorite jam.

Raspberry Mascarpone Matcha Roll Cake

Sponge cakes in Asia contain less fat and sugar than Western versions, giving them a lighter, fluffier texture. This texture makes them the perfect foundation for a slightly more indulgent, Western-style filling. The light sweetness of the raspberries, the rich creaminess of the mascarpone, and the slightly bitter earthiness of the matcha all work together beautifully.

PREP TIME: 20 minutes

COOK TIME: 12 minutes, plus assembly time

TOTAL TIME: 1 hour

SERVES: 8

OCCASIONS: high tea, birthdays, bridal showers, weddings

FOR THE MATCHA SPONGE CAKE

3 large eggs, room temperature

100 grams (½ cup) granulated white sugar

60 grams (¼ cup) whole milk

15 grams (1 tablespoon) canola or vegetable oil

¼ teaspoon kosher salt

½ teaspoon pure vanilla extract

75 grams (½ cup) cake flour

2 teaspoons matcha

Confectioners' sugar for rolling

1 First, make the sponge cake. Preheat the oven to 350°F (177°C) and line a baking sheet with parchment paper or a silicone baking mat.

2 Separate the egg whites and yolks.

3 With a hand mixer in a medium mixing bowl, beat the egg yolks with 25 grams (2 tablespoons) of the sugar on medium-high until the mixture lightens in color, about 2 minutes.

4 Add the milk, oil, salt, and vanilla extract and continue beating to combine until a light-yellow batter forms, about 2 minutes.

5 Sift the cake flour and matcha and fold both into the custard.

6 In another medium mixing bowl, beat the egg whites and the remaining 75 grams (6 tablespoons) of sugar on high until stiff peaks form, about 3 minutes.

7 With a spatula, gently fold one-third of the meringue into the batter until just incorporated.

8 Repeat twice more with the rest of the meringue.

9 Pour the batter onto the baking sheet and spread it into an even layer.

10 Bake until the middle-top of the cake springs back when gently pressed, 10 to 12 minutes.

11 Remove from the oven and let it cool for about 3 minutes.

12 While the sponge cake is cooling, generously dust it with confectioners' sugar.

(recipe continues)

FOR THE RASPBERRY MASCARPONE

120 grams (½ cup) heavy whipping cream

90 grams (⅔ cup) confectioners' sugar

½ teaspoon vanilla extract

250 grams (1⅔ cups) mascarpone cheese, room temperature

235 grams (¾ cup) raspberry preserves

Fresh raspberries for serving

NOTES

Fold the meringue gently into the batter to avoid deflating it too much.

The filling will start separating after 3 days, so enjoy soon after baking or wrap slices in plastic and freeze for up to 2 months. Thaw frozen slices in the fridge overnight before serving.

13 Cover the cake with a clean kitchen towel and, using the towel to keep the cake in place, flip it upside down.

14 Peel off the parchment paper or gently remove the baking mat.

15 From the long end, gently roll the cake tightly into a roll, sugar side in, and set aside.

16 Next, make the raspberry mascarpone. In a medium mixing bowl, add the heavy whipping cream and sift the confectioners' sugar into it.

17 With a hand mixer on medium, beat until stiff peaks form, about 2 minutes.

18 Add the vanilla extract and beat to incorporate, about 30 seconds.

19 Add the mascarpone and continue beating to combine, about 1 minute.

20 With a spatula, swirl the raspberry preserves into the filling.

21 To assemble, unroll the sponge cake and spread the filling on it, leaving about ¼ inch of space around the edges.

22 Gently but firmly roll the cake back up, keeping the roll tight.

23 With a sharp knife, cut into slices and serve with fresh raspberries.

TIP: When slicing the cake, wipe the knife between cuts to achieve clean slices.

White Sesame Batons

I'm going to share a secret with you: I didn't love sweets until I turned 30. A switch flipped from "Yeah, they're OK. I love making and sharing them" to "My second stomach houses only dessert!" Asian cuisines have lots of rolled cookies closely resembling tuiles, the classic French wafer cookies. These Asian cookies taste beautifully crisp and, you guessed it, not too sweet. The sesame seeds in these batons make them incredibly fragrant. Enjoy them on their own or dip them in Lychee Buttercream (page 38) or White Chocolate Ganache Filling (page 42).

PREP TIME: 25 minutes

COOK TIME: 15 minutes, plus cooling time

TOTAL TIME: 1 hour

MAKES: 24 small batons

OCCASIONS: Lunar New Year, Mid-Autumn Festival, high tea, Christmas

60 grams (¼ cup) salted butter

Egg whites from 2 large eggs

65 grams (⅓ cup) granulated white sugar

35 grams (¼ cup) all-purpose flour

45 grams (½ cup) toasted white sesame seeds

NOTES

Chilling the batter makes it easy to spread the ovals thinly on the baking sheet. The batons will harden as they cool. In an airtight container at room temperature, the batons will stay fresh for 2 days. They don't freeze well, so enjoy them soon after baking.

1 In a large microwave-safe bowl, microwave the butter on high for 15 to 20 seconds to melt it, then let it cool for 3 minutes.

2 While the butter is cooling, preheat the oven to 375°F (190°C) and line two baking sheets with parchment paper or silicone baking mats.

3 Into the butter, stir all the ingredients except the sesame seeds with a spatula until well combined.

4 Refrigerate the batter for 10 minutes.

5 Onto the prepared baking sheets, spoon the chilled batter into 24 ovals, 12 on each baking sheet. Using the back of a spoon, spread the thin, crêpe-like batter into ovals about 2½ inches long. Space the ovals evenly to allow for slight expansion.

6 Sprinkle the sesame seeds on top of the ovals.

7 One sheet at a time, bake until the edges slightly brown but the middles remain relatively pale, 6 to 8 minutes.

8 Remove from the oven, carefully turn the hot cookies over, and immediately roll into batons with sesame seeds facing out. Move quickly since the cookies are very thin and set fast, and they will crack if they cool down too much.

9 Let cool to room temperature on a cooling rack.

White Sesame Batons

Salted Egg Yolk
Shortbread Cookies

Salted Egg Yolk Shortbread Cookies

In college, when I was selling handmade jewelry, one of my customers, Wendy Lee, became a good friend. She has supported all my businesses. She also adapted my shortbread recipe into these sweet and salty cookies. I still can't believe that I didn't come up with the idea first, but thankfully Wendy likes to share!

PREP TIME: 15 minutes

COOK TIME: 18 minutes, plus chilling and cooling time

TOTAL TIME: 1 hour 30 minutes

MAKES: 12 cookies (3-inch diameter)

OCCASIONS: high tea, book club, Mid-Autumn Festival, Christmas, New Year's Eve

---

225 grams (1 cup) salted butter, room temperature

90 grams (⅔ cup) confectioners' sugar

½ teaspoon vanilla extract

4 Salted Egg Yolks (page 53)

300 grams (2 cups) all-purpose flour

NOTES

Shortbread dough and baked cookies both freeze well. Wrap in plastic and store in freezer bags for up to 3 months. Roll the dough into a log and slice before baking, or cut the dough into shapes before freezing. Bake from frozen.

1   In the bowl of a stand mixer fitted with the paddle attachment, cream the butter and sugar on medium until light and fluffy, about 3 minutes.

2   Add the vanilla extract and 2 of the egg yolks and continue beating to combine until the homogenous mixture looks relatively smooth, about 2 minutes. A few chunks of egg yolk are OK.

3   All at once, add the flour and mix on low until the dough just comes together, about 2 minutes.

4   Halve the dough and roll each half to ⅓ inch thick.

5   Wrap the rolled-out dough in plastic wrap and refrigerate for 30 minutes.

6   Preheat the oven to 375°F (190°C) and line a cookie sheet with a silicone baking mat.

7   With the bottom of a heavy mug or glass, crush the remaining 2 egg yolks. Aim for small, consistent chunks.

8   When the dough has finished chilling, cut it into desired shapes and place the raw cookies on the prepared cookie sheet. Reroll the scraps to use all the dough.

9   Press the crushed egg yolk crumbs into the tops of the cookies.

10 Freeze the raw cookies for 10 minutes.

11 Straight from the freezer, bake until slightly browned around the edges, 16 to 18 minutes, rotating halfway through.

12 Remove from the oven and let cool on the cookie sheet or, for crispier cookies, on a wire rack.

S'mores Cupcakes with Toasted Marshmallow Buttercream

When Netflix cast my friend Sonia Kim and me for the baking show *Sugar Rush,* neither of us had baked a cake from scratch before. We were cookie people, not cake people! Within a few weeks, though, we baked more than 50 *pounds* of cake for practice. We sliced it all into large, ugly chunks, stuffed them into gallon-size plastic storage bags, and took them to work. Anyone adventurous enough to take a free bag of cake was welcome to it—and it all disappeared within hours. Over time, that practice cake became a vanilla bean cake recipe that has morphed into . . . the base for these cupcakes. Surprise!

PREP TIME: 25 minutes
COOK TIME: 25 minutes, plus cooling and assembly time
TOTAL TIME: 1 hour 30 minutes
MAKES: 12 cupcakes
OCCASIONS: cookouts, summer, fall, Christmas, camping, weddings

FOR THE S'MORES CUPCAKES

225 grams (1½ cups) all-purpose flour

400 grams (2 cups) granulated white sugar

65 grams (¾ cup) unsweetened cocoa powder

2 teaspoons baking soda

1 teaspoon baking powder

1 teaspoon instant coffee or instant espresso

1 teaspoon salt

240 grams (1 cup) buttermilk

120 grams (½ cup) vegetable oil

2 large eggs, room temperature

2 teaspoons vanilla extract

1 cup hot water

1. First, make the cupcakes. Preheat the oven to 350°F (177°C) and line a muffin tin with paper liners.

2. In a large mixing bowl, stir together the flour, sugar, cocoa powder, baking soda, baking powder, instant coffee, and salt until well combined.

3. Add the buttermilk, oil, eggs, and vanilla extract and mix until just combined.

4. Add the hot water to the mixture and stir until smooth.

5. Fold the chocolate chips and mini marshmallows into the batter.

6. Pour the batter into the liners, filling each two-thirds of the way full.

7. Bake until a toothpick inserted into the center comes out clean, 20 to 25 minutes.

8. Keep the oven on and let the cupcakes cool in the tin to room temperature before frosting.

9. While the cupcakes cool, make the buttercream. Line a baking sheet with parchment paper.

10. Place the mini marshmallows on the baking sheet and broil until golden brown, 1 to 2 minutes, making sure they don't burn. Set aside to cool.

11. In the bowl of a stand mixer fitted with the paddle attachment, beat the butter on medium speed until light and fluffy, about 2 minutes.

(recipe continues)

100 grams (½ cup) semi-sweet
chocolate chips

100 grams (1 cup)
mini marshmallows

Mini marshmallows for garnish

Graham cracker pieces
for garnish

1 chocolate candy bar, broken
into pieces, for garnish

FOR THE TOASTED
MARSHMALLOW
BUTTERCREAM

50 grams (1 cup) mini
marshmallows

115 grams (½ cup) salted butter,
room temperature

120 grams (½ cup) whole milk

240 grams (1⅔ cups)
confectioners' sugar

½ teaspoon vanilla extract

½ teaspoon salt

12 Add the milk and continue beating until well com-
    bined, about 2 minutes.

13 Gradually add the confectioners' sugar and continue
    beating until the mixture becomes smooth and
    creamy, about 2 minutes.

14 Add the vanilla extract and salt and beat until well
    combined, about 2 minutes.

15 Fold the toasted marshmallows into the butter-
    cream, reserving some for garnish.

16 Mound or pipe the buttercream frosting onto the
    cupcakes.

17 Garnish with the reserved toasted marshmallows
    and pieces of graham crackers and chocolate candy
    bar and serve warm.

TIP: Use an ice cream scoop to mound the buttercream onto the cupcakes.

NOTES

In step 4, hot water activates the cocoa powder, inten-
sifying its flavor.

The toasted marshmallows are going to make the
buttercream frosting a little chunky, and that's OK!

VARIATION

If you have a kitchen torch, you can use it to brown the
mini marshmallows for the buttercream.

Black and White Icebox Cookies

When I was growing up, my dad satisfied the collective family sweet tooth by buying us panda icebox cookies. They tasted firm and buttery and looked adorable. As an adult, I long for the treats that my dad bought for my mom, grandma, and me. This recipe doesn't create pandas, but these cookies are easier to put together and still look cute.

PREP TIME: 30 minutes

COOK TIME: 15 minutes, plus resting time

TOTAL TIME: 2 hours 45 minutes

MAKES: 24 cookies

OCCASIONS: Holiday cookie plates, cookie exchange, picnics, bake sales, hiking, Valentine's Day, Christmas

---

225 grams (1 cup) salted butter, room temperature

200 grams (1 cup) granulated white sugar

1 large egg

2 teaspoons vanilla extract

450 grams (3 cups) all-purpose flour

½ teaspoon baking powder

28 grams (¼ cup) unsweetened cocoa powder

VARIATION

By playing with the doughs, you can create a ton of different patterns. For stripes, cut the dough into strips, layer them, and cut without rolling.

1. With a hand mixer in a medium mixing bowl, cream the butter and sugar until light and fluffy, 2 to 3 minutes.

2. Add the egg and vanilla extract and continue beating until well combined, about 2 minutes.

3. In another medium mixing bowl, stir together the flour and baking powder.

4. Add the dry ingredients to the wet ingredients and mix until just combined.

5. Halve the dough.

6. Leave one half as is and add the cocoa powder to the other half. Mix until well combined.

7. Roll out both sets of dough to a rectangle, about 5 by 7 by ¼ inch.

8. Stack the rectangles and, from the long side, roll into a log.

9. Wrap the log tightly in plastic wrap and refrigerate for at least 2 hours or overnight.

10. When ready to bake, preheat the oven to 350°F (177°C) and line a cookie sheet with parchment paper or a silicone mat.

11. Slice the log into 24 cookies, each about ¼ inch thick, and place on the prepared cookie sheet.

12. Bake until the plain edges turn lightly golden, 12 to 15 minutes.

13. Let the cookies cool on the cookie sheet for 5 minutes before transferring to a wire rack to cool completely.

NOTES

The parchment paper hanging over the sides of the baking dish allows you to remove the caramel easily after it sets. When the liquid caramel boils, the mixture may bubble and spit, so be careful. Store wrapped caramels in an airtight container at room temperature for up to 3 weeks or in the freezer for up to 3 months.

Matcha Caramels

When I was selling cookies on Etsy, I came across a confectioner who created beautiful blocks of caramel cut into slices and wrapped in parchment with twisted ends, like Christmas crackers. They looked classy, minimal, and timeless. I ordered Earl Grey caramels, honey caramels, and chocolate caramels. Receiving that package felt like a warm hug from a friend. The Earl Grey caramels, my favorite of the three, inspired me to create these Asian-flavored treats.

PREP TIME: 10 minutes

COOK TIME: 15 minutes, plus cooling time

TOTAL TIME: 5 hours 30 minutes

SERVES: 8

OCCASIONS: Christmas, Chinese New Year, Valentine's Day, Mother's Day

355 grams (1½ cups) heavy cream

1 teaspoon matcha powder, sifted

200 grams (1 cup) granulated white sugar

100 grams (½ packed cup) light brown sugar

80 grams (¼ cup) light corn syrup

½ teaspoon salt

1 teaspoon vanilla extract

15 grams (1 tablespoon) salted butter, room temperature, plus more for greasing

1 Line an 8-by-8-inch baking dish with enough parchment paper to hang over the sides and grease the paper.

2 In a small bowl, whisk together one-quarter of the heavy cream and the matcha until smooth.

3 Fit a medium saucepan with a candy thermometer that doesn't touch the bottom of the pan.

4 In the saucepan over medium heat, combine the matcha mixture, the rest of the heavy cream, the sugars, and corn syrup. Stir constantly with a wooden spoon until the sugars dissolve completely. The mixture will look thick and cloudy.

5 As the mixture comes to a boil, brush the sides of the pan with a pastry brush moistened with water to prevent sugar from crystalizing on the sides of the pan.

6 Cook, stirring occasionally, until the temperature reaches 250°F (121°C).

7 Remove from the heat immediately and stir in the salt, vanilla extract, and butter.

8 Pour the liquid caramel into the prepared baking dish and tap it on the counter a few times to pop any bubbles and smooth the surface.

9 Let the caramel cool and set, uncovered at room temperature, for at least 5 hours or overnight.

10 When the caramel has set, lift the parchment paper to remove it from the pan.

11 With a sharp knife, slice the block into rectangles or squares.

12 Wrap any caramels that you don't eat right away in parchment or wax paper.

Raspberry Swirl Marshmallows

My constant drive for efficiency has turned into a game: "How little equipment and time do I need to make this?" Homemade marshmallows intimidated me for years. Boiling sugar, measuring its temperature, and beating it into egg whites? That didn't sound like fun! But a TikTok video of a London shop cutting giant marshmallow squares finally convinced me to give it a shot. This recipe achieves consistent results without a candy thermometer. Always grease whatever utensils you use to move your marshmallow mixture—otherwise, it will stick to everything!

PREP TIME: 15 minutes

COOK TIME: 10 minutes, plus cooling time

TOTAL TIME: 8 hours 30 minutes

SERVES: 8

OCCASIONS: Lunar New Year, Valentine's Day, Christmas

---

180 grams (¾ cup) cold water

20 grams (1½ tablespoons) plain, unflavored gelatin

200 grams (⅔ cup) light corn syrup

400 grams (2 cups) granulated white sugar

½ teaspoon kosher salt

Neutral oil for greasing

Confectioners' sugar for dusting, rolling, and storing

80 grams (¼ cup) raspberry jam or preserves

1 In the bowl of a stand mixer fitted with the whisk attachment, add 120 grams (½ cup) of the cold water and stir in the gelatin. Set aside to bloom.

2 In a medium saucepan over medium-high heat, combine the light corn syrup, sugar, and the remaining 60 grams (¼ cup) of the water and stir constantly until the mixture comes to a vigorous boil.

3 Let the mixture boil for 3 minutes *without* stirring.

4 Remove from the heat immediately and pour into the stand mixer bowl.

5 Add the salt, whisk on medium speed for 2 minutes, then increase speed to high for 8 more minutes.

6 While whisking the marshmallow cream, grease an 8-by-8-inch baking dish with oil and dust it with confectioners' sugar.

7 When the marshmallow cream has tripled in size and looks shiny and thick, it's done. This takes approximately 10 minutes. Then, with a spatula, gently swirl in the jam.

8 Pour the marshmallow cream into the prepared baking dish. Dust the top with more confectioners' sugar.

9 At room temperature, let the marshmallow cream set, covered with plastic wrap and undisturbed, for at least 8 and up to 16 hours.

(recipe continues)

VARIATIONS

Use different jams, such as mango or plum, to switch up the flavors. To create another layer of texture and flavor, drizzle or coat the pieces in the flavored white chocolate of your choice.

10 Remove the marshmallow block from the dish and, with a greased knife, cut the block into squares or rectangles.

11 Roll the pieces in more confectioners' sugar, squish, and enjoy!

TIPS: Not using a candy thermometer can result in undercooked or overcooked syrup. Test the sugar for readiness by dropping a small amount in a glass of cold water. The sugar blob should hold its shape and, when you remove it from the water, feel gently pliable. It shouldn't dissolve (undercooked) or become rock hard (overcooked).

NOTES

In step 4, the mixture will bubble violently and grow, which is good! In step 5, your stand mixer might heat up and protest because the cream becomes sticky and difficult to mix after a few minutes. Keep going! When adding the jam, don't overmix. You want to see some swirls.

In case you skipped the headnote, *always* grease the utensils that you use to cut or move the marshmallow mixture to prevent it from sticking to everything.

At room temperature, store marshmallows in an airtight container—with a little more confectioners' sugar to coat the container and absorb moisture—for about 1 week or frozen for up to 3 months.

Acknowledgments

This cookbook stands as a heartfelt testament to the collective effort and inspiration of many wonderful individuals. My deepest appreciation goes to my parents and grandma for nurturing my love of food, using it as a conduit for connection and joy, and for challenging me to do better at every turn. Thank you for helping me develop skills that I could depend on when life gets tough.

To my extended family, friends, and colleagues—past and present—you are my pillars of support, eager taste testers, and empathetic listeners during the chaos and isolation of entrepreneurship and life. While our paths may not always intertwine, and some journeys have come to an end, I always will remember and cherish your impact on me. Thank you.

I am incredibly grateful for the entire *Matcha Meets Macaron* team who made this book possible. Lary and Barb, thank you for finding me and believing that I had a story to tell. Huge thanks to James J. from Countryman, for advocating for me and the vision of this book. Your expert guidance and patience working with a first-time author like me are deeply appreciated. Allison, thank you for shepherding the book through the design process, resulting in beautiful styling and layouts. Special thanks to Kara, who brought my recipes to life with captivating photography, and much love to James d'S., who helped capture the day-to-day processes of my work and private moments with my family.

To the Borderlands family, fellow dessert enthusiasts, and home bakers: this book wouldn't exist without you. May each recipe within these pages sweeten your celebrations, imprint cherished memories, and leave an indelible mark on those fortunate enough to share in the joy of your creations.

Index

Page numbers in *italics* indicate illustrations.